CONFESSIONS *of a*

Childfree WOMAN

a life spent swimming against the mainstream

CONFESSIONS *of a*
Childfree WOMAN
a life spent swimming against the mainstream

Marcia Drut-Davis

Confessions of a Childfree Woman: A Life Spent Swimming Against the Mainstream
©2013 by Marcia Drut-Davis

ISBN-13: 978-0615819235
ISBN-10: 0615819230

Cover design by Derek Murphy of bookcovers.creativindie.com
Author photo by Wendy Conrad of WLC Photography
www.wlcphotography.com
Text design by Lisa DeSpain of www.ebookconverting.com

Some names have been changed to protect privacy.

Dedication

As the *60 Minutes* crew packed up their last suitcase of wires, microphones and lights, Rhea, my mother-in-law, looked at me. Her aging mouth quivered, accentuating the red lipstick traveling along fine wrinkles.

"Why did you get married if you never wanted children?" she said, fighting back tears. "What if this is a mistake? How will you feel when you're old and can't have children?"

This memoir is a look back at how I made the difficult choice not to have children, and the consequences of my national exposure on *60 Minutes*, as well as an exploration of regret. It's written for anyone who chooses not to procreate, feels pressured to have more children, or may be unsure of their wants. This book offers an understanding of the very real consequences of not raising children, even in today's society which claims to accept childfreedom.

I dedicate this book in loving memory to my mother Juliette, father Nathan, and stepfather Sam. They gave me the courage to step up to the challenge of the words, "To thine own self be true."

Table of Contents

Foreword by Bonnie Weiss

This book is ultimately about courage, the courage to take a look at conditioned ideas and ask difficult questions. In a world where so much isn't working, it's wise and prudent to take a bold look at certain values we hold dear and challenge those that are not in line with our true beliefs. It's important to support crusaders who do the challenging. Marcia Drut-Davis is one of these people.

This book is an honest and forthright exploration of all that goes into the decision to become a parent—or not to, and the reality of living with the consequences. Marcia is a gifted story-teller who pulls you into her world with engaging images of her family, touching memories of her relationships, and poignant accounts of her struggles with stepparenting. She is candid and often brutally honest about her feelings as she explores from all angles the choice to be a parent.

I am a psychotherapist who works with Internal Family Systems Therapy (IFS), a unique model created by Richard Schwartz, Ph.D. From this work, I know that we're all complex beings who have many different voices or "parts" inside of us. These parts are born from childhood efforts to cope with our upbringing, take on various roles, integrate into the culture, and function effectively in society. There are also voices that speak for our own unique preferences and longings. The first step in becoming a conscious adult is gaining awareness of these some-times conflicting parts of ourselves.

We have parts that assume we will carry out the expectations of our cultural background: fall in love, get married, and have children. There may also be parts that have other ideas and therefore, resist living out the status quo. The feminist movement spoke to this issue. It fought long and hard to make sure that today's women feel entitled to a variety of options in the world, a variety of internal voices.

In order to make a decision about a weighty issue, it's critical that all parts of one's self have a seat at the table of consciousness and thus, a chance to be heard. Whether we hold these discussions in our heads or commit them to paper, this process of fully acknowledging all of our voices helps us to make choices that reflect our deepest values and forge our life path. The result is greater peace within. One significant measure of maturity is our ability to live with the internal and external consequences of our decisions. Marcia embraces both. Her memoir thoroughly explores the vicissitudes of the choice not to parent. She checks and rechecks her decision against societal pressure, maternal inclinations, and biological clock-ticking. The reader is granted access to the recesses of her mind as time marches on and her life and body change.

This work is the study of a carefully made decision—a decision with consequences. It was not an easy road, but it was traveled with humor, courage and pluck. I celebrate this work and believe that it will give pleasure and insight to those who read it, wherever in your life or decision-making you may be.

"The secret of health for both mind and body is not to mourn the past, not to worry about the future, but to live in the present moment."

-Buddha

1
In the Beginning

It was 1954, and I was twelve years old. I clearly remember how the opaque curtain felt as I stood behind it with my back to the window, facing the living room. Slowly, I began walking, the curtain pulling in the opposite direction. A musty smell entered my nostrils. It needed washing. I didn't care. As I continued to step, stop, step, stop, I mimicked the wedding walk down the imaginary aisle in our living room, savoring each moment of my fantasy wedding day. My hands clutched an imaginary bouquet of fragrant white flowers. I heard the band playing "Here Comes the Bride." I heard the crinoline rustle under the billowing dress.

I walked in slow motion flanked by my mom on one side and dad on the other, as the Jewish tradition dictates. Mom wore a pink dress with a matching coat. She nodded to the left and right recognizing family and friends. Dad stood stoically by my side as he fought to contain his emotion. People were whispering how gorgeous I looked. There was a sea of faces I had known growing up: family, friends and neighbors all staring approvingly.

I saw some amorphous person standing under the chuppah. His face kept changing from one handsome male actor to another, all those heartthrobs that populated my pre-teen fantasies, whose photos were plastered all over my bedroom walls. Like so many of those posters, my husband-to-be was tall with dark hair, piercing brown eyes and a sculpted body. He wore a perfectly fitted black tuxedo. I kept walking towards him, watching his eyes brim over with tears that fell gently down his face. I knew he was thinking, "I'm so lucky. Look at my gorgeous bride!" Although, in all honesty, I didn't much care who the groom was. It wasn't as important as the soft veil over my head, gorgeous flowers in my hand and the fairytale dress that surrounded me.

The fantasy felt real. I was breathless.

The fantasy abruptly ended as I reached the end of the curtain. It slipped off my head gently and returned to its rightful place beside the window. I stopped short. No more veil. No more wedding. I was back in our fourth floor apartment in the Amalgamated Housing Project in The Bronx.

"Marcia!" Mom yelled. "Go wash your hands. It's almost time for dinner."

I could smell the fragrant aroma of Mom's Sunday brisket simmering in tomato sauce and onions. Dad whistled as he listened to his favorite classical music station in the kitchen. He pointed and waved his imaginary conductor's baton, bringing the horns in at the right moment of a Beethoven symphony. Neither of them saw me in my fantasy wedding. Neither of them imagined their daughter anticipating her future nuptials at the tender age of twelve. They still viewed me as their little girl.

It would be another ten years before they saw the real wedding. The fantasy became a reality in a lavish two hundred person sit-down roast beef dinner, replete with white-gloved waiters, eight-piece band, and female singer in a black sequined, low-cut dress. My groom was very handsome in his black tuxedo. My bridal dress mimicked the fantasy of my youth with a huge gathered bustle shaped like a flower. I wore a veil that ended at the tip of my hands, topped by a sparkling crown.

Many years have passed, and I only vaguely remember the details of that long-awaited day. I do, however, have the exalted wedding album with the frozen images, those Kodak moments I thought I'd want to remember forever.

On the day I received my wedding album, there was a coupon attached for a free 11x10 photo of our firstborn child. I remember thinking, "Baby? Are they kidding?" I couldn't imagine a baby so early in the marriage. It would, of course, be a part of our life, I reasoned, but not now.

I had just started teaching second grade. I still had to learn how to wash the bathroom floor. Cooking presented another challenge! I didn't know much about sex, although it was fun to learn. Baby? I still had to experience the art of making love.

To be brutally honest, I had never been aglow with the idea of procreating. I was disturbed by the thought of my vagina stretching like a huge rubber band, squeezing something the size of a bowling ball out of my uterus. My mom had explained how babies were born, with a faraway look that I couldn't quite read. The details of her seventy-two-hour labor during which she screamed "Kill me! Please! Now!" didn't land with a warm fuzzy in my heart. Of course, she said I was worth all the pain and discomfort she suffered. Somehow, I couldn't bring myself to believe her.

When I was fifteen, my only sibling, Robin, was born. Mom had remarried after divorcing my father when I was fourteen. My stepfather, Sam, had never had children or been married despite the fact that he was tall, well-built, and very handsome. My mother wanted another child with him. It was difficult enough adapting to a new father, new neighborhood in Manhattan, and new high school. Now I had to get used to a new life in the house as well. From the beginning, it all felt like too much.

When my baby sister came home from the hospital, I was jolted by the realities of raising a child. It seemed to me that there were simply not enough hours in the day to care for her special needs: preparing formula, boiling bottles, burping her then cleaning her spit-up, giving baths, changing diapers, visiting the doctor, attending to her primal screams during the night, dressing her for outside, undressing her when she came back, and walking the floor at night once she started teething. My eyes grew wider and wider every day as the realities became clearer.

My mom had gone back to work two weeks after Robin's birth. She was an important lady: the first American woman in the 1950s to run a successful TV repair business. She had started as a secretary, and spent her lunch hours watching the men fix TVs. Eventually she learned enough to do it all herself, and finally got the notoriety as a capable businesswoman she had craved all her life. *TV Guide* ran a story about her. Nobody guessed her career on *What's My Line?* She appeared on the cover of *Radio Electronics Magazine*, posed at a workbench, facing the back of a TV, holding a tube and smiling. The title of that article read, "Did She Get the Job? No, She Got the Company."

Mom was an enigma in the '50s and '60s, when moms stayed home, wore white aprons and baked sugar cookies. In her youth, she was drop-dead gorgeous. She had an oval face with high cheekbones and deep, brown eyes. She would wear large brimmed hats, white gloves and sexy outfits that hugged her trim, curvy body. She would become heavy in later years, but for now, she was a movie star. Somehow, she managed to be a mother and a businesswoman, too. She enjoyed being a mother, but returning to her work was a necessity. She loved the challenges of owning her own business and, perhaps more importantly, welcomed a reprieve from the dual career of raising her baby daughter.

Mom placed Robin in the loving care of our housekeeper, Clara. She would arrive every morning in eager anticipation to care for my baby sister. Upon entering the nursery and seeing Robin's tiny arms outstretched from her crib, Clara's smile would spread wide across her dark ebony face, radiating genuine love.

She would pick her up tenderly, bring her to her large breasts, and coo, "Good morning, my sugar."

Her sugar could do no wrong, not ever. When Robin was a toddler, I saw her throw a crystal ashtray across the room. It hit the ground and shattered.

"Aw, sugar! That's not nice!" Clara said. "Come here and let me give you a hug and a smooch." Robin ran into her arms, content in the understanding that her next naughty adventure would also be overlooked.

I loved my baby sister with all my heart. She was, however, one huge pain in my teenage ass. Unlike Clara, my fuse was short when baby sister tested my boundaries. She would steal my lipstick and hide it in her dollhouse. It became routine to find missing personal property in that dollhouse: jewelry, nail polish, makeup, my phonebook. At first, it was cute. Then it got old. She would interrupt me when I spoke with my friends on the phone. She wanted me to play with her all the time. Clara did, and Robin couldn't understand why I couldn't. She spilled my favorite perfume on a homework assignment, forcing me to retype the entire thing that night. She wedged herself between me and my boyfriend when he came to take me out.

"Hi, David," Robin said.

"This is Julian," I answered.

"Where is David?" she asked innocently. "I like him more because he plays with me."

To an eighteen-year-old, this was not funny.

Mom spent a lot of time with Robin when she wasn't working. She delighted in having a baby again. However, she didn't have the same energy at thirty-eight that she had had for me at twenty-two. I observed her leave for work in the morning—eagerly, I thought—and come home exhausted. Her business was in The Bronx; we lived in Manhattan. She had to use public transportation. Many evenings, she would return after we had

17

eaten dinner. I would warm her food while Robin waited for playtime with Mommy. By the time she played with Robin, gave her a bath and put her to bed, she had only energy enough to read a few pages of her book before falling soundly asleep. Sam or I would move the book from her chest to her nightstand, gently so as not to wake her. On the nights she came home after I was in bed, I would drift away to the clip-clop sound of her heels on the kitchen floor. I remember thinking that she moved slower at night than she did in the mornings.

I began to question if I could work all day, come home and still have enough energy to take care of my child. Would I be able to afford a housekeeper? Would I have a mate equally interested in the task?

Sam cherished being a first-time dad at the age of forty-two. He adored me and his baby daughter, delighting in her adventures. He would bounce Robin on his knee, laughing his booming laugh while he prepared my favorite breakfast: scrambled eggs and burnt toast. (Burnt was the only way he could make it.) Robin was daddy's little girl, and had him wrapped around her little finger. Sam and Mom both spent many weekends taking her to the park, pushing her on the swings, or going shopping with her. They treasured these moments while I slept late, watched TV, or spoke on the phone with my friends. I often wondered if they themselves longed for such luxuries.

Robin listened to both of them carefully. When they were around, she knew her limits. One look from my mom stopped her dead in her tracks. A firm "No" from Sam was all it took.

Of course when I babysat, she never listened. She taunted me and seemed to do exactly the opposite of what I asked her to. Once, I remember feeling particularly annoyed by her antics. I put her to bed.

"GO TO SLEEP!" I barked.

I could feel my pulse in my temples. About ten minutes passed. The house was quiet, and I breathed a sigh of relief. As

I curled up on my bed to watch a favorite show, Robin ran into my room screaming, "Na na nana na!! Nanny nanny poopooo!"

I pushed her so violently, she fell and split her lip.

"I hate her. Come home now!" I screamed into the phone at my mom.

"Marcia, she's just a child," Mom quietly replied. She always lowered her voice when she disapproved. I learned to dread that whisper. I didn't know it then, but I would hear it many times in the years to come for the hard decisions I made.

I still wince at that memory. As adults, I've asked Robin many times if she remembers. Thankfully, she swears she doesn't. Although I only wounded her feelings—the small cut on her lip, I tended to with concern and was relieved when it healed perfectly—I felt as if I had abused her. I had no understanding of how to deal with the frustrations of taking care of a child. I wondered how I would handle frustrations with my own child. And more importantly, would I want to?

Robin's daily needs were frustrating, relentless, and sometimes frightening. There were two emergencies that landed her in the hospital. Both occurred while I was babysitting. The first time, she shoved a button up her nose. It all turned out fine in the end, but riding to the hospital in the cab was terrifying. I was convinced the button would become lodged in her little brain, and it would be my fault. The second time, she dislocated her shoulder falling from the monkey bars at the playground. There was another frantic rush to the local hospital. Her tears and sobs overwhelmed me as I cradled her in my arms. My own tears felt warm on my cheeks. Meeting my mom at the hospital was a relief; she took over as caretaker, and got me off the hook. Although I had gone through the motions, I couldn't help but feel that I had failed when Robin needed me most.

I remember feeling that maybe, just maybe, I didn't want to have children. I didn't like the hard work. This job was seven days a week, twenty-four hours a day, with no days off. Parenting wasn't at all the way it was depicted on TV, the largest problem solved within a half-hour time frame, and it wasn't like playing house on the stoop of my friend's Saxon Avenue house. Even then, I often preferred the role of the child. Mothering—even pretend mothering—was just too much work. What I liked best about playing house was that when I got bored, I simply stopped playing. Try that in real life!

I marveled at my mother. Her professional life seemed to energize and excite her. Her success gave her a sense pride and accomplishment. I loved listening to her stories about the challenges she faced, and enjoyed my friends' surprised reactions when they learned of her career. But I felt sorry when she came home exhausted, only to face the hard work of caring for her little girl. It wasn't all Robin; I also made demands on my mother. She typed my term papers, went to all my school events, and sewed the hems on the jeans that never fit (I was small for my age!). Would I do the same for my children? Would I prefer to have a career, not in addition to parenting, but instead?

I would have these thoughts, and dismiss them just as quickly. That kind of thinking was sure to lead to years of expensive, gut-wrenching psychotherapy. It was, after all, my biological destiny! It was what I was made for! It was why I would get married! There were logical steps to be taken. I would first find the man, say "I do," then start a family like every other woman I knew. The instinctive urge to procreate would dominate at the right age with the right man, wouldn't it?

2
Men Minus Babies

I met my first husband Jack through his aunt, our neighbor on the 6th floor of our apartment building in Riverdale, New York. He had me at first wink. He was suave and very handsome, with an athletic build, cleft chin, sunken cheeks, and two dimples that appeared when he spoke. His smile made me feel vulnerable and a little embarrassed, and made all my friends swoon with envy.

"He's gorgeous!" my best friend gushed after meeting him.

He certainly was. Integrity? Honesty? Faithfulness? Those characteristics were important too, I told myself, but looks took precedence. I was shallow, and didn't yet know what I wanted or needed. When Jack looked at me with a combination of lust and tenderness, I felt simultaneously turned-on and safe. I felt naked despite being properly dressed (which I always was). I got lost in his stares and knew from his reactions he was equally excited. I desperately wanted to have sex with him, but wouldn't; good Jewish girls didn't have sex until they were married. He told me not to worry: he wouldn't take advantage of me. I believed him.

Jack was a flatterer. When he took me out, he always had something complimentary to say: "Hi, baby. You look adorable." I melted every time he used the word "baby." Nobody had ever used that word with me before.

Jack never went unnoticed. He had a larger-than-life personality, a presence that lit up a room the moment he entered. A wave of his hand, a flick of his cigarette, an outburst upon seeing someone he knew, and all eyes were on him, just the way he liked it. He sought out attention relentlessly and, although I too had an outgoing personality, his totally dominated. Eventually, I learned to sit back and allow him to perform. With his arms around my waist and sliding to my backside, I was just fine. Let him perform. I was his "baby."

I was relieved to be his girlfriend. I was the only one of my friends not planning a wedding, pregnant, or raising their first child. If this relationship didn't lead to a marriage proposal, I was sure the title of "Old Maid" would be bestowed upon me at the tender age of twenty. I had had three previous boyfriends, and they had all left me. One said he wasn't ready to settle down. Another told me his heart belonged to another girl. The third suddenly stopped calling, although I thought we were in love. So it had to work out between Jack and me, it just had to.

I longed to buy my own brides' magazines and pick out my own china pattern instead of agreeing with my friends over their choices. I had at least four different bridesmaid's dresses hanging in my closet. I hated them all. I wanted my own wedding gown, and the ability to choose my own awful fashion statements for my bridesmaids to wear.

And children would come in time. Jack was beautiful, after all, and marrying a beautiful man meant having beautiful children. The thought caused me discomfort, I'll admit, but I believed wholeheartedly that, someday, I would come around.

"I'll want kids when I marry Mr. Right." I thought, and it certainly seemed like Jack was him. Yes, I would want to make a little person out of him and me. Of course I would want that.

As our dating escalated and our relationship became more serious, Mom started to find things about Jack she didn't like. She thought he was pretentious and loud. She hated to see him dominate my usually outgoing personality. She didn't trust him, she told me.

She caught him in outright lies. His aunt had given away the fact he was a salesman, not the manager of his department as he had claimed.

When confronted, he laughed it off. "You heard me wrong!" he said. "I said I'm *going* to be a manager soon."

Although he was a successful salesman in a prestigious Manhattan clothing firm, he wasn't the doctor or lawyer my mom had wished for me. Nice and Jewish weren't enough. He traveled a lot. Mom was sure he had other girlfriends along his route. I'm sure she was right. She didn't like that we fought a lot. She was right about that too. He had to have things his way, no comprising, and he did. I defended Jack as best I could, and attacked Mom in the process. "You just want to keep me as your little girl forever," I accused. "I'm a woman! I can make my own choices."

"Okay, miss woman!" Mom shouted back. "As long as you're living with me, you can meet him in the apartment lobby. He makes my skin crawl."

From then on, Jack was under strict instructions to ring our bell from the lobby. I would use the intercom to tell him I was on my way down.

I had to prove to Mom that Jack was my soul mate and, more importantly, that I was right. So what if she didn't approve of him? He was the one. I would be with him forever. He would bring out my dormant desire to have kids. We would start a family, and live happily ever after.

I remember the night I got engaged. He didn't get on one knee. He didn't ask me to marry him, or place the ring on my finger. He didn't even wrap the damn ring case. He sat across from me in a pizza parlor, wearing a smug smile as he produced his grandmother's ring. Though I felt vaguely uneasy, even had a moment of queasiness, I took the ring and placed it on my left finger.

I decided I would change the ring—the setting was too old-fashioned for my taste. I decided I would change the groom into a more receptive listener, a real partner, a better man. I would do all that and the instinctive urge to procreate would follow, my lingering doubts about the parental lifestyle would melt away. I would change myself from a single woman into a wife and mother.

I brought Jack home with me, and flashed my mom the ring.

"Jack," she said carefully, "if Marcia chooses you, I accept you. Let's call a truce." They hugged. I swear, I heard the refrain from "Kumbaya."

There was an engagement party, lots of presents, and a surprise bridal shower in Manhattan. I spent my days and nights looking at the china patterns, writing Thank You cards for all the gifts, and looking forward to being a married woman.

Jack and I never discussed children. We both assumed we would be parents, that children would be a part of our life. That was, after all, the natural course of events.

"First comes love, then comes marriage, then comes Marcia with a baby carriage," I had chanted while jumping rope as a child.

We didn't discuss how or when we would try to have children, how we would raise them, or even if we were parent material. What would we do if our child was unhealthy? What would we do if were unable to have children? Would we be open to adoption? These vital issues didn't seem as important as choosing the first song we would dance to at our wedding reception. I chose "More," the popular theme song from "Mondo Cane." The last line, "No one else could love you more," was my mantra.

ᔦᕽᕽᕽᔧ

Three weeks after our wedding, Jack went off to Germany to serve in the Army Reserves. I cried and waved as he boarded the plane, turned and blew me a kiss. He looked terrific in his uniform.

Walking to my car, alone, I drove directly to Mom's. She opened the door and embraced me.

"I feel so sad and alone," I gushed. "I love falling asleep in Jack's arms and seeing him every morning"

It was a blatant lie. The truth was that marriage to Jack had revealed itself to be nothing at all like I had fantasized or expected. He would wake every morning, urinate in the bathroom, and smoke a cigarette before returning to our bed where he would nudge me for sex. He would enter me, wanting a quick release, planting wet kisses on my lips with foul, smoky breath.

Never once, after we both came home from work, did he help me with dinner, or anything for that matter. While he sat on the couch puffing away, sipping a drink, and talking on the phone, I set the table, prepared the food, and cleaned it up. In his defense, men didn't do much of that sort of work back then. (Hell, they don't do much of it now, relatively speaking. According to the 2010 U.S. Census, there are 5.1 million stay-at-homes moms and only 154,000 stay-at-home dads. I rest my case.) He had watched *Father Knows Best*, and agreed with Ralph of *The Honeymooners* that a woman's place was in the kitchen. Lived experience, I was learning, was quite different from the scenes we enjoyed on TV.

Jack did hold me while we fell asleep. That part, and that part only, was true.

My life with Jack consisted of waiting for arguments, which came like clockwork. We once argued about what movie to see. He wanted a blood-and-gore film; I wanted a serious drama that would touch my heart. Unable to compromise, Jack lost it. He grabbed my beloved dog, Brandy, and ran out of the apartment, threatening to dump her in the Hudson River. I chased him to the parking lot only to see him driving away with Brandy peering out the car's back window. I felt sick. When he returned two hours later with my dog, thankfully, unharmed, he just laughed.

I began to have anxiety attacks, periods of restricted breath and dizzy spells, which became more frequent as we continued our ongoing dance of dysfunction. I felt completely out of control, and utterly trapped. I couldn't tell anyone about Jack's cruel treatment of me. If I told Mom, it would validate her warnings; she would be right, and I would be wrong. If I told my friends, I would have to face their pity and disapproval. If I confronted Jack, I feared the stigma of divorce and the seemingly insurmountable challenge of starting my life over. So I kept my unhappiness to myself, clinging to the naive belief that I would eventually change him and then my life, my family, could really begin.

Around our first wedding anniversary, I stopped taking birth control pills. It wasn't to see if we could get pregnant; far from it. I kept a growing cache of articles about how birth control pills could lead to breast cancer and other serious health issues. Jack supported my decision, suggesting we try for a baby. I declined adamantly.

"I'm not ready," I told him matter-of-factly. It was the truth. I still felt like a child myself, unsure of how to take care of my own needs, let alone another human being's. What I didn't tell him was that the thought of making a baby with him left me short of breath.

He agreed to use condoms, but didn't know how to use them correctly. They often burst.

When I missed my period, I went to my OB/GYN.

"Looks like you're pregnant," he announced triumphantly.

I was stunned and terrified. Pregnant? Me, a mother? Jack, a father? Although our relationship had been better lately, it was far from perfect. He still didn't understand how to be a partner, or how to treat me as an equal. During a heated argument a few weeks before, he had picked me up and put me in a garbage pail on our street. As I struggled to get out of the putrid-smelling pail, I had felt like a piece of garbage, discarded, completely and utterly worthless. What would he do to our child when she was naughty? I couldn't bear to think about it.

Despite these disturbing thoughts, I ate more consciously, my baby in mind, subsisting on fruits, vegetables, and pre-natal vitamins. Maybe this baby would change our relationship for the better, the way I had been told babies do. A baby would help Jack mature. He would want to work on our marriage. We would be drawn closer. I kept touching my flat stomach, wondering when I would feel that feathering my friends had told me about: my baby moving in my belly.

Jack was ecstatic. He had fathered a child. He was a man! Of course it would be a boy. He strutted around like a peacock.

A week later, I started staining a dark brown substance. I was afraid something was wrong, so I called my doctor.

"I just got the results of your pregnancy test," he said. "It's negative. I'm sorry. But you're young. I'm sure I'll be seeing you soon as a pregnant mommy." The staining, as it turned out, was my period.

I hung up the phone and slumped into a chair. I was deeply saddened. My son or daughter was not inside me. My womb was empty when it should have been full. I had failed as a woman.

Slowly, it dawned on me: I was relieved. I didn't have to worry about the inconveniences of pregnancy, the horrors of childbirth, the stress of protecting a life, or the damage that Jack would almost certainly inflict. My doctor had told me not to eat anything starting with a "p": peanuts, pretzels, potato chips, or pickles. They contained too much salt. I immediately ran out and bought a slice of pizza. I was celebrating. Bringing a child into this world, into a dysfunctional home, was no longer my concern, at least for now.

Two miserable years later, Jack was transferred to California for a management position with his clothing company. Sitting next to him on the jumbo jet, the realization that I couldn't live with him another nanosecond took hold. I got up, got out, and called my mom.

"I can't do it! I can't move to California. I can't be with him anymore."

I braced myself for the "I told you so" I was sure was coming. Instead, there was a long silence, followed by the last words I expected, or wanted, to hear.

"Go with your husband," she said finally. She spoke so quietly, I could barely hear.

Six months after moving to California, I was still suffering in this marriage. Jack often came home smelling of booze and perfume. On a hunch, I followed him to a Palm Springs hotel where he was attending a convention, or so he said. I caught him with a woman who had followed him to the West Coast from New York. Apparently, they had enjoyed an affair while he worked in Manhattan. His late night meetings had been with her.

Jack was the first of three marriages. Without a doubt, I had many valid reasons not to have a child with him. It would have been wrong, for both of us and for that innocent child. Looking back, I'm grateful that things worked out the way they did.

The day after our divorce was finalized, Jack remarried. He had a son with her who became, of course, a doctor.

ॐ

After I divorced Jack, I didn't think about children. I put the issue out of my mind. There was no marriage connection and therefore, no pressure to procreate. I felt at ease, free of the troubling thought that I wasn't cut out to be a mom, that I was different from every woman I knew. I didn't hear my biological clock ticking. I didn't feel any urge to wind it. I would have children someday—what choice did I have?—but that day was not today. I went from the single sexual experience with Jack to being single in the time of free love. AIDS and sexually transmitted diseases were unheard of. The next few intimacies I experienced were in service of my sexual and emotional education, rather than fulfilling some destiny for motherhood.

Ken, my first lover after Jack, showed me what tenderness and excitement felt like, both in the bed and out. It was a wonderful awakening.

In the end, I broke his heart. He was serious about me. I was ardently into learning more about myself, men, and life, not necessarily in that order. After three years of hell, I wanted nothing to do with commitment. He wrote a lovely piano piece for me entitled "My Love." On the corner of the handwritten sheet music he proclaimed, "I wrote this for you before I met you. It tells you what you are." His devotion scared me. He told me, on more than one occasion, that he wanted to marry me and give me a baby as an expression of his love. The word "baby" brought back the confusion and conflict I had experienced as a married woman. I ran as fast as I could into another relationship.

Peter paddled over to me in a friend's community swimming pool I used to frequent. His arms and legs hung out of a black tube as he splashed towards me. Obviously, I was his target. He had a round face, green eyes and wet brown hair plastered to his forehead. On his upper lip was a slight beading of perspiration from the warm California sun. I wore a sexy swimming suit with a plunging V-neck of see-through black netting. It was far from the little girl look I used to embrace. Closer and closer he paddled, finally stopping directly in front of me at the side of the pool.

It was small talk at first.

"Hey, you just move into the community?" he asked. He had a thick Boston accent that I thought was cute. Still, he was a stranger, and I kept my distance.

"I don't live here," I replied.

"Know someone here then?"

"A friend."

"Who's the friend?" he questioned, pausing in his paddling to splash his back. I started to think he was a bit nosey. "Is she hot?" And pushy. He never waited for my answer. "I love hot women. Older ones especially. Last night at a swinging party, I had the sexiest older woman who scratched my back. See?" He turned to show me three angry-looking marks on his left shoulder blade. "What a woman! Ever swing?"

That was it. I was officially disgusted by this man. Here he was, asking personal questions and sharing inappropriate information with a total stranger. I excused myself, telling him that I needed to find my friend. He got the hint immediately.

"Have I shocked you?" he asked. He had. He knew he had. "Hey! Sorry if you're offended. Let me make it up to you. How about dinner?"

I can't imagine why I accepted. In all likelihood, it was a combination of wanting to give him the benefit of the doubt, curiosity, and loneliness. Having moved 3,000 miles away from family and finding it difficult to make many new friends, nights were solitary. I would often aimlessly wander a nearby supermarket just to be around people. I decided it might be fun to go out with Peter. It would certainly be better than walking around a supermarket touching the broccoli.

The next night, Peter arrived well-dressed, with a hint of a suntan from the pool and some lingering Aramis aftershave. He took me to a popular restaurant where a live four-piece band was playing. People seemed to be enjoying themselves both on the dance floor and at their tables. The smell of sizzling steaks told my stomach I was hungry.

We had a wonderful leisurely meal with lots of laughter. We also found we danced well together. He didn't mention swinging again until the end of the evening. It was I who questioned his lifestyle. The wine may have played a role in my brazen interrogation.

"Why do you want multiple sexual partners?" I asked. "Isn't one at a time enough?" He smiled and looked away for a moment, presumably thinking about how to respond.

"We just enjoyed a steak dinner," he finally said. "Can you imagine having a steak dinner every night? Sometimes I like lobster, cod, or chicken. I love women. I love their differences. I never want to know just one."

I reacted defensively. "But don't you want to settle down, have a family, and know the value of a close, secure relationship?" I heard myself parroting the values I had been taught—and which still exist today—failing to acknowledge that I myself had questioned these values often.

"Children? Me? Never. Why would I want kids running around, demanding my time, money, and energy? Kids are not in my future. They're too much work!" I agreed, of course, but I wasn't yet ready to admit it. I felt a knot form in the pit of my stomach, a hard kernel of truth demanding attention. "You were married," Peter went on. "How did that secure thing work out for you?"

I had never heard anyone speak like Peter, so direct and without artifice. "That's hurtful. You sound selfish," I snapped.

"Why?" he retorted. "Because the truth hurts? Because you've been raised to believe if a man is in love with you he should want to give you a baby? Selfish? If I can't take care of my own needs, who can?" He smiled at me then, toothy and self-satisfied.

"This will never work out," I told him.

"That's ridiculous! We could have a wonderful time together. You don't even know how I can make love with you yet!"

"Take me home," I barked. I couldn't believe the balls on this man.

He sighed and asked for the check. We sat in icy separation on the car ride home. Nothing more was said until we arrived at my apartment.

"Listen, I'm sorry if you're angry," Peter said as he parked his car in front of my building. "I'm attracted to you. I like your spunk. I even find your naivety appealing. Maybe I can broaden your horizons, get you out of this old-fashioned thinking. You want an honest friend, right? Maybe I can even get you to try swinging. You might like it."

Like hell I would. I thanked him for dinner, got out of the car, and slammed the door telling him I could get to my apartment alone.

I went inside, took off my clothes, and took a long bath. I was fuming. I wanted nothing more than to wash this man away from my body and thoughts. But I kept thinking about what he had said. Wasn't he articulating what I thought but wouldn't admit? Didn't I question whether I wanted to raise kids? Why had I reacted so angrily?

The phone rang. I got out of the tub and grabbed a towel as I picked up the receiver.

"Hey, Marcia. It's me, Peter. Listen, I hope you aren't upset. I just called to tell you I'm sorry if I offended you. I guess I came on too strong."

I had to laugh. I had never met anyone like Peter. I never would.

"Apology accepted. And yes, you do have unusual beliefs," I said.

"I'm simply looking for a woman who can keep an open mind. Women I meet are so brainwashed. They have defined goals: get married, stay faithful, and have kids. Boring!"

Something resonated deep within me. He made sense. He intrigued me. I agreed to see him again and, over the next several months, our friendship continued to grow. We had met in the right place, at the right time. After my experience with Jack, I was hungry for friendship, not romantic commitment. Peter welcomed that. Although he was blunt, I eventually found his outspokenness amusing and enlightening. This man was a free spirit. I began to enjoy him wholeheartedly.

He introduced me to the fun of sex. He was a damn good teacher, patient and attentive. Our relationship was based on honesty, which I appreciated most of the time. Certain information, like his women who gave good head or invited anal sex, I wished he would keep to himself. I learned not to ask what he did on his business trips. If I didn't ask, he didn't share his intimate escapades. I knew he wasn't faithful to me, although I was to him. That was the nature of our arrangement, and it worked for us at the time. Eventually, we moved in together and loved each other monogamously for one year. It had been Peter's idea.

One morning, after breakfast, Peter heaved a deep sigh. He rubbed his hands together nervously, bouncing one leg on the ball of his foot. It wasn't like him to be so uptight. I knew something was up.

"Marcia, this isn't working," he began. "I love you but I feel suffocated."

"Why?" I asked weakly.

"I don't like being with only one woman. I want more freedom."

"I know that!" I exclaimed, now on the verge of tears. "Have I ever asked you to do otherwise?"

"You haven't. I appreciate that. This past year has been terrific, but it's time for me to move on. I'm not going to marry you. I'm not going to give you children. I'm not what you want."

Was that true? A husband and children and all the trappings of married life, was that what I wanted?

Either way, that life wasn't for Peter. There was no argument, no push-and-pull. It was simply time for him to leave and for me to get on with my life. And that's exactly what we did.

Peter and I remain good friends. We call each other on birthdays, and catch up in between. He never married, had kids, or stayed in any monogamous relationship. He remained a contented bachelor.

❦

Right around the time that mine and Peter's relationship ended, I got an animated phone call from my Aunt Frieda.

"Listen," she said breathlessly. "I found your next husband! He's gorgeous, has money, and he's Jewish!"

I was able to appease Aunt Frieda for a while. It was easy. The man she had in mind, Warren, lived in New York. I was 3,000 miles away. Still, she insisted I send her a recent photo she could pass on to the groom-to-be. When she heard I was planning a trip home, she insisted we meet. Warren was very funny when he called.

"Marcia? This is Warren. Listen, your Aunt Frieda is driving me crazy. I understand you're coming to visit soon. Let's agree to meet, tell her it just wasn't meant to be, and thank her for trying. That'll stop this insanity."

We were surprised when we met. There was instant chemistry between us. We laughed at how Aunt Frieda had relentlessly pursued her matchmaking quest, and admitted that we were glad she did. (Looking back now, I realize that my Aunt Frieda was the precursor to Match.com. What vision!) Warren came to visit me in California. I returned to New York to see him. For several months, we traveled back and forth on many red-eye flights. Although I still hated flying, I tolerated it for Warren.

When I was offered a position substitute teaching on Long Island, I took it. There was nothing keeping me in California. I feared the constant earthquakes and hated the phony behavior of women my age who were more interested in starving their bodies than feeding their minds. Besides, I missed my friends and family back east. Of course, I was eager to be near Warren and curious to see where this new relationship would lead me.

Our relationship was off to a great start. Warren wasn't rich like Aunt Frieda had thought—she heard this from Warren's mom, who lied—but he was gentle, kind, and predictable. My mom loved him. My dad liked his sense of humor. My friends thought he was perfect for me.

Not long after, Warren and I moved in together. He was working hard, running a clothing store in Selden, Long Island, and I was a popular substitute teacher working almost every day. I kept the children happy and on task, and always got through the teachers' lesson plans. Parents wrote glowing letters to the principal stating how happy their children were when the permanent teachers were absent. Although there weren't any full-time teaching positions available, I was slated for the next opening. I felt safe and happy in the life I had chosen.

"I think it's time we take this relationship to the next level," Warren said casually over breakfast one day. That was my marriage proposal. No kneeling, no ring, no nothing. Again. Although slightly disappointed—would I ever get a romantic proposal? a nod to the domestic fantasies I had yet to let go—I agreed to marry him.

It was a small June gathering in my mom's backyard. I carried daisies, and recited my vows: "I recognize we love each other but don't belong to one another. We are unique individuals who will maintain our individuality and not succumb to being a reflection of the other person's wants and needs. We will be aware of the challenge to be open and honest as we grow old together. I accept you just as you are and will not try to change you. I love you." It was very '70s, very hippy-ish, and well-received by our guests. The ordained leader of the Ethical Humanist Society asked our guests to share their feelings about the union. People openly expressed their love for both Warren and me, and wished for us a long and happy life. We presented Aunt Frieda with a homemade matchmaker award. Everyone laughed, Sam loudest of all, of course. Mom wiped away a tear of joy and relief. I was now 31. She wanted a grandchild.

Warren and I settled into a sweet, predicable lifestyle. We opened our little apartment to friends and family, hosting dinner parties and special occasions. We spent our weekends relaxing together, reading books and seeing movies. Soon we welcomed a stray dog we named Buffy. Her antics were adorable. It was an added responsibility—all the walking, feeding, playing, and pampering—but one we were more than happy to take on. Our marriage had no highs or lows. It was even as can be, calm and secure. Warren came home to me every night. We were a content family, Warren, Buffy, and I.

When the clothing store failed, Warren started his own business in home inspections. Although we were far from rich, we were able to purchase our first home. It was a fixer-upper disaster replete with flying cockroaches, spray painted walls that read, "Vito Sucks!", and a front porch on the verge of collapse. When my mom visited for the first time, she could hardly speak. That was unusual for her. I'm not sure if she wanted to laugh or cry. On second thought, she definitely wanted to cry.

By the time Warren's parents Ben and Rhea arrived, they were impressed. Warren had made the house presentable. He reinforced the front porch, painted over the graffiti in a warm brown color, and replaced the old stained carpet with a new shag rug. I decorated with antiques and paintings to make the place feel like home. My in-laws surveyed the house smiling. They couldn't stop telling us how proud they were of all we had accomplished in only two years of marriage. Then it started.

"So?" Rhea began, blinking her eyes rapidly, the way she did when she was nervous or excited. "I guess that extra room upstairs will be your nursery. When can we expect the happy news?" She moved closer to me and patted my belly. "Start practicing!"

Warren and I looked at each other in disbelief. His parents had never pressured us to have children. Why now? Warren and I had never discussed having kids. Although I had felt a vague sense on more than one occasion that we should have been talking about it, I welcomed silence around the whole unsettling matter. I truly believed I was the only woman on the planet who wasn't sure whether she wanted children. I had never considered my husband's thoughts on this important issue. I now know it was benign neglect. I loved the way we lived. Teaching was wonderful. A full-time position was right around the corner, and Warren's business had started to flourish. We could even afford a vacation. We had friends we saw often, and free time to spend as we pleased. If Warren said he wanted to have children, I didn't know how I would react.

"Give us a chance, will you?" Warren chuckled, clearly uncomfortable. I sat back and breathed more steadily. "Between the business and the house and—"

"Babies bring their own luck," Rhea interrupted, a bit miffed. "You can handle it. Your father and I were poor when we had you!"

"Dinner's ready," I announced, changing the subject. Warren gave my hand a squeeze.

Warren and I never discussed that troubling moment with his mother. We simply went on with our lives, no children in sight.

❧

Warren and I had grown accustomed to watching all of our married friends struggle with their children's never-ending wants and needs. We listened to complaints about the difficulties of juggling their careers and home lives. Money was a constant challenge. Still, they seemed eager for us to join them in the insanity, asking often when we planned on "settling down."

At the same time, they saw the appeal of our lifestyle. A few admitted outright that they were jealous of our weekends. We could do anything we wanted or nothing at all. They envied our ability to take nearby trips to the Poconos, or Hunter Mountain, or the farms east of us where we bought ripe peaches and cooked them for homemade jam. They longed to sleep late, enjoy a leisurely breakfast, and return to bed for sex (always with protection!), as we often did. Afterwards, we would read, putter around, nap, or watch old movies.

Needless to say, our friends' weekends looked very different from ours. Their kids had all kinds of commitments: play dates, birthday parties, baseball games, ballet or karate lessons, and shopping for clothes. As parents, their time was not their own.

The parents we knew did sometimes manage to get away, but even then, responsibilities loomed. A simple dinner date at our house meant planning well in advance, finding, paying, and trusting a babysitter. If their children got sick, they canceled. If they did manage to escape, to sit down with us for some adult time, it was not uncommon for our guests to leave early. Inevitably, they would be too tired to make it through the evening, or the babysitter would call with a question, or they would panic for no reason at all. Just thinking about living that way left me feeling exhausted.

During these dinners, however brief, our friends would share their triumphs as parents: seeing their child's first solo bike ride, sending off their kindergartner to his first day of school, or hearing their toddler speak her first whole sentence. At times, it was endearing. Other times, it was annoying. We were happy for them, really, but we had no interest in all their stories.

Their need to share endless baby photos was totally frustrating.

"And here's Lucy taking her swimming lesson. Isn't she too cute for words?" a friend gushed.

I wanted to shriek, "Yes, she's adorable but, please, no more! I can't take another picture! One is okay, but twelve? It's the same pool, the same kid, the same goofy smile!" I felt like I was drowning in those pictures.

Warren and I endured endless slideshows and discussions of their children's adventures because it would have been cold-hearted not to. But what could we say besides, "That's interesting," "Oh? How exciting," and "Wow, good for you"? These were not the sort of conversations that stimulated our minds. We wanted to discuss current events, politics, books and plays, and we wanted to socialize with people who wanted that too.

"Is it just me or do you feel we have nothing in common with our friends anymore?" I asked Warren.

He nodded in agreement. "Their lives are just different. Their kids come first. We'll have to join the parent club to fit in."

When I heard those words, I cringed. Was this it? Was Warren about to say we should start trying for a child?

"Maybe we need to find friends who don't have kids," he said. I breathed a sigh of relief.

Unexpectedly, around this time, I received a book in the mail from my father's wife. Vivian was a librarian. Books were her passion. She knew all the new releases that were flying off the shelves or reserved months ahead. "Thought you two may find this interesting," Vivian's note read. I picked up the book and read the title: *The Baby Trap* by Ellen Peck. Vivian and I had never been close. She was an overbearing know-it-all. Still, this title intrigued me. Baby? Trap?

I immediately sat down at our kitchen table and started reading. Three hours later, I had read the book cover-to-cover. I was amazed, excited, and empowered by the concepts I had just digested. So parenting was a choice. I was free to choose motherhood—or not. It was entirely up to me. I thought about Peter who had said the same thing. Perhaps I needed to hear it from a professional, an authority, rather than a boyfriend. Whatever the reason, I got the point now. Not only was it okay not to have children, it was safer in a lot of ways. Peck warned that parenthood could be dangerous to one's health and well-being. I had never thought about it in this way. I felt educated, alive, and freer than I had in a long, long time.

"What's for dinner?" Warren asked when he got home from work. Usually, I would have a meal simmering on the stove. Not tonight. I had been busy reading a book that would change both of our lives.

"I think we need to talk about this," I said, handing him the book.

"From the look on your face, I'll finish it as fast as I can," he said.

He read Peck's book in only a few days. We sat down and, for the first time, openly and honestly talked about whether or not we wanted to have children.

"I'm relieved," Warren said. "I don't want kids. I never have." He reminded me of a song he had written for me when we first got together. It told our story, and ended with an image of me cradling our baby in my arms.

"I remember how touched I was," I said.

"I thought it was poetic," he admitted. "I thought that's what you wanted to hear. Honestly, I was afraid you wouldn't marry me if I didn't want kids. You never brought up the subject, so I didn't either."

"Can you imagine if I wanted kids and you didn't?" I asked, shaking my head. "Then what would have happened?"

"I probably would have agreed to it and gone through the motions of being a father even though it's not at all what I want." I wondered in that moment if my biological father had done that very thing. He and his second wife remained childfree. "Parenthood is too much work. I like things the way they are now."

We talked for a long time. I told him about my childhood—my parents' love and commitment, the games we played, the trips we took, the luxuries we enjoyed—and what a joy it had been. I had no need to relive that time through my child. I had been then and was now completely satisfied. I also shared my negative experiences with Robin, that unpleasant initiation into the world of parenting which I had absolutely no desire to repeat. Warren explained that he had never taken to kids, never had so much as an impulse to be a father. It just wasn't for him. He reminded me that we were still struggling financially. According to *The Baby Trap*, the cost of raising just one child was staggering—$19,000 to $25,000—and it didn't even include the cost of sending a child to college! Today, it's upwards of $200,000. Finally, the decision had been made: I would not have children.

At the end of the book was the phone number of the Manhattan chapter of N.O.N., the National Organization for Non-Parents. I called. My life would never be the same.

3

60 Minutes

My heart raced. I slowly dialed my mother-in-law Rhea's number. The line rang for what seemed like an hour before she answered.

"Hi, Mom. It's Marcia. Do you have a few minutes? I need to talk." I wondered if she could hear my heart beating wildly.

She said she had the time and asked me to wait a second while she turned down the stove—homemade chicken soup, no doubt. I heard her scurrying around, clanking a spoon, and moving her chair as she sat down at the kitchen table. "Okay, I'm listening."

I took a breath and continued. "Warren and I want to talk with you and Dad tonight. It's very personal. We don't want to interrupt you if you have company or made plans for this evening." There was a pause, then an affirmation. They had no plans and would be home.

"Oh my God!" she shouted as if something had just occurred to her. "Is anything wrong with you or Warren?"

"No! We're both healthy and happy. It's not anything like that," I replied. I proceeded with caution, choosing my words carefully. We had been warned not to say too much on the phone. "Mom, we're involved in a new direction in our life. We want to tell you and Dad about it in person."

"Wonderful!" she answered. "You sound very animated and excited. Come on over. Can't wait to hear about it."

In truth, I wasn't animated or excited; I was scared, especially when I asked if she would mind the crew of *60 Minutes* tagging along.

There was silence. I could picture her blinking her eyes a few times, tapping her fingers on the table like she did when she was nervous.

"Is it drugs?" she asked finally. "Are you involved with using or selling drugs?"

"Absolutely not!" I snapped.

"Well, is it pornography? Group sex? Are you a stripteaser or a pole dancer?"

I stoically replied that it was none of the above, wondering how she knew about pole dancing.

"Marcia, are you a lesbian?" she whispered. The question startled me. I wondered why she hadn't asked if Warren was gay.

"Nothing at all like that," I said.

"You're both Communists?"

"No, Mom," I laughed. "Listen, this may be a difficult experience. Are you sure you want to do this?"

I almost hoped she would say, "On second thought, no." Instead, she said that she and Ben would be waiting in their apartment. "What could possibly be worse than what I listed?" she asked.

If only she had known.

❧

Everything happened so fast. Maybe that was a good thing. If I had really stopped to think about the ramifications of what I was doing, I wouldn't have agreed to anything. That night we were going to tell Warren's mom and dad, once and for all, to leave us alone because we had chosen never to have children. We were tired of the constant not-so-subtle hints and probing questions about when we would give them a grandchild. We would make this announcement, and we would not be alone. The crew of *60 Minutes* would also be there. Ultimately, millions of viewers would be privy to this intensely personal experience.

It happened this way. A few months earlier, Warren and I had joined the now defunct N.O.N. (National Organization for Non-Parents), a cutting-edge organization headed by the outspoken Ellen Peck, author of *The Baby Trap* and the High Priestess of the Childfree. We looked forward to attending our first meeting, eager for the opportunity to meet people whose feelings about having and raising children mirrored our own.

We weren't sure who these childless people were or if they would accept us. The ride on the Long Island Rail Road from Centereach to Manhattan gave us ample time to talk.

"You know, we may not like these people," Warren suggested.

I agreed it was a distinct possibility. Images of free-loving Woodstock hippies danced in my brain. Back then, it was a popular belief that people who didn't want kids were aloof and immature. I'm embarrassed to admit that I internalized that misperception, while of course clinging to the belief that Warren and I were the exception to the rule. I was relieved to discover that most N.O.N. members were not, in fact, freaks of nature, or cold, selfish people who only cared about their personal wealth or hedonistic pleasures. They were engaged, mature decision-makers, intelligent and interesting; a diverse cross-section of people hailing from all types of backgrounds. They shared stories about their professional lives, higher education, travel, volunteer work, and the pursuit of artistic hobbies like writing poetry. They validated their own reactions to the pressure to procreate, and laughed at the excuses they kept giving to stop the relentless questioning. They felt at ease in the meetings, but admitted to the difficulty of being honest with friends and family. One couple told people they couldn't conceive. Their families sent them to fertility clinics all over the world. This couple shared their guilty feelings about accepting free travel! We all laughed.

When Ellen announced she was arranging the first national N.O.N. convention, I volunteered to help her. It was an exhilarating time for me. I met famous people I had read or heard about like Isaac Asimov, the prolific science fiction writer, and Hugh Downs, co-anchor of *Good Morning America*. Ellen arranged for *60 Minutes* to film a segment at that first convention. It would be great publicity for our cause and a way to reach others feeling the pressure to raise children.

The convention was a blessing to Warren and me. We met more childless people from all over the United States. N.O.N. chapters were cropping up from the East to the West Coast. Even I had committed to starting a Long Island chapter. We were giddy with excitement and warm feelings as we heard others talking about the childfree lifestyle. We no longer considered ourselves a childless couple. We were a childfree family.

With these new sensations of freedom and relief came a growing feeling of annoyance. Why was it okay for people to ask us when we were going to have kids, but if we dared to ask them why they had had kids, it would be considered an affront? In all of my years of education, why hadn't I ever heard that parenting is a choice, not a requirement? Sex education taught how the sperm travels through the vagina to reach the sacred egg, but never touched upon the possibility that we may not want children, or that a childless lifestyle was a viable option and an opportunity for a richly rewarding life. Never was there any mention of whether or not you should have children, could have children, or would even want to. The same holds true today.

I thought back to many of my students' parents, their short-comings and blind spots. How many of them were overbearing? How many refused to accept substantiated facts about their offsprings' educational challenges, such as low IQ, ADHD, or Dyslexia? Perhaps they were angry that their children were not living up to their high—oftentimes, too high—expectations. Perhaps they saw their children's limitations as a gross reflection of themselves.

One irate father said, "I never had such low grades!"

"You're not your son," I gently replied.

How many parents didn't take time to read with their kids, or learn how to listen to them? How many compared their child's accomplishments to a sibling, pitting one against the other? Sadly, many of my students' parents were guilty of mental and physical abuse.

I once had to stay at school past 10:30 p.m. because one of my students confided that her mother's boyfriend was sexually abusing her. She was twelve years old. Her mother defended the boyfriend. This same mother also hit her son on the head with a hammer in a fit of anger. Those two kids were eventually taken from their home, separated, and forced to live in a succession of foster and group homes for years. After Warren and I were approved by social services, I took them into our home on the weekends. The boyfriend eventually admitted his guilt and was sent to jail. The mother begged her children for forgiveness.

I felt honored to provide a soft place for these two children to land. They knew they had an advocate in me; at least that. I stuck with them through all the years of tremendous challenges, following their progress and checking in to make sure they were safe and happy. No holiday went by without them visiting me.

No birthday passed without gifts, hugs and love. I stood proudly watching as both children got their high school diplomas and went on to graduate college. To this day, I consider them family, although I'm not their parent and do not want to be.

As the convention wound down and Warren and I said our goodbyes, Ellen brought over Marion Golden, her guest and the producer of the *60 Minutes* segment being taped. Apparently, someone had suggested that Warren and I were ready to tell our parents the truth about our decision.

"When will you do that?" Marion asked.

"Very soon," I said, not entirely sure where this conversation was headed.

"Would you consider taping that with us, tonight, after the convention?" she asked. "It could help so many explore the beauty of honesty. It's an important piece and will make this puzzle whole for our viewers."

She got to me. I was elated by the deliciously freeing idea that I wouldn't have to hide my true feelings anymore. I was ready to shout it from the rooftops. Warren was skeptical at first, but ultimately agreed.

I phoned my mom from the convention to see if she and Sam would agree to being interviewed. They weren't home. That's when I called Warren's mom and got her okay. We were given money to take a cab from the convention site in Manhattan to Rhea's and Ben's apartment in Queens. All too soon, we arrived at their building. The ride in the elevator seemed endless. Neither Warren nor I said a word. We were both lost in separate fantasies of the scene that was to follow, and all that would be revealed. I knew this would not be easy on any of us. We had always enjoyed a close relationship with Warren's parents. Would this change everything? Would my in-laws hate me? Although I had fears, I held the naive belief that they would come to accept and support our choice. We would explain, and they would agree.

I was greeted by a bewildered Rhea who seemed cautiously curious about what was going on.

"I can't believe this," she said. "Wait till you see our kitchen." She took our coats, and led us in to see for ourselves.

The crew had already transformed the kitchen into ground zero for taping. The kitchen table had been cleared of personal belongings. Where keys and magazines had once lived, we saw wires, monitors, and a collection of strange-looking electrical equipment. Men were scurrying around inside. Others walked back and forth between the kitchen and living room, which was bathed in a sea of lights. I could feel the warmth they generated. I noticed one microphone suspended over the couch, and my stomach flipped.

Thankfully, there was no time to discuss anything more with Rhea. Marion Golden arrived shortly thereafter and ushered us into the living room. Ben sat in a chair beside the couch, completely expressionless and smoking a cigar. I gave him a quick hug and sat on the couch with Warren. His mom joined us. Someone came and powdered our faces with a touch of makeup. I heard someone else say, "Check! Check! Check!" and a flurry of static followed.

I felt like a movie star. I watched the audio technician adjust the microphone. He looked positively bored. He didn't seem to care about the sounds emanating from my heart into his headpiece. He was there to do his job and nothing more. I wondered if he had been briefed on the topic of the segment. So what if I was about to announce my deepest, darkest secret to the world? Big deal! He probably thought we were a pair of hedonistic slobs who were getting a kick out of breaking our parents' hearts while enjoying the notoriety.

One-by-one, the crew exited the living room, leaving only the producer and the camera person. Both were listening intently to their headpieces. I could see the people in the kitchen watching tiny versions of us on monitors. There was total silence, then:

"Thanks for allowing us into your home," Marion said. "I'm sure this will be an interesting discussion. Forget about us. Just talk."

The strong smell of my father-in-law's acrid cigar smoke assailed my nostrils. I felt a wave of nausea, and began to feel very nervous. I was mostly aware of the heat from the intense lighting, and the quizzical looks on my in-laws' faces. Their eyes darted around the room, filled with confusion, fear and worry. I had a strong desire to suck my thumb in a fetal position and have at least six biological children with two adopted from a third world country; one would, of course, need extra care due to a physical defect.

I had been all for this but now, I couldn't find one word to say. My hands were shaking. My crotch started sweating. I couldn't breathe. Little stars danced in my vision. I thought I might pass out, and half wished for it to bring this horrifying experience to an end.

Thankfully, Warren began. "You know Marcia and I have been going to Manhattan a lot lately, right?" Warren's parents nodded. More silence. "Do you know why?"

"No," Mom said. More silence. This was going to be a long night.

Warren went on to tell them that we volunteered to help a newly established educational organization. I noticed a little perspiration forming on my husband's upper lip. The hand holding mine was hot and sweaty.

"Warren and I know how much you want a grandchild," I said quietly, finding my voice. Mom and Dad looked at each other and smiled. "We're sure you would make wonderful grandparents. But we've made the choice not to have children."

Their smiles instantly vanished. Their faces turned to stone.

"We feel pressured by everyone," Warren said. "Mom, you pat Marcia's belly, for crying out loud, tell her to go home and practice. We're happy just the way we are. It's that simple."

Tears were starting to form in my mother-in-law's eyes. Still, not one word from either of them.

"This new organization has opened us to the need for honesty," Warren continued. Apparently, he had found his voice too. "It's not fair for you to expect grandchildren when it's not going to happen. We know this is very disappointing. Still, we're asking for your love and support."

There was (excuse the expression) a pregnant pause. They both stared at us. I had learned, in a sales course I had taken, that if you're selling something and there's a pause, the one who speaks first loses. I waited for what seemed an eternity. I was determined not to lose.

Finally, my father-in-law spoke. "I suppose you have the right to make your own choices," he said flatly.

I felt a rush of relief. My mother-in-law was now openly crying, staring down at her folded hands. My father-in-law continued, puffing more intensely on that cigar. As it turned out, my relief was short-lived.

"I repeat, you have a right to choose your own life. However, this is such an immature decision. I'm sure you'll change your minds."

Then came the verbal assault. They both listed all the reasons we would regret this decision: the joys of watching our child grow up, the knowledge that we would live on in another, and the contribution to our family tree. They asked all the usual questions that I would come to know with great annoyance and, later, understanding. Why did we get married if we didn't want kids? Who would take care of us when we were old? What would we do with our lives? Then my mother-in-law went in for the kill. She looked directly at her son and wiped away her tears.

"Warren, what did I do wrong in raising you? How can you be so selfish?"

My father-in-law set down his cigar and fixed Warren with a piercing stare. "If we had felt the same way, where would you be right now, son?"

Warren and I answered all of their questions with respect. They had a right to know why parenting wasn't for us: the hard work, endless challenges, financial responsibilities, our desire for travel and a freer lifestyle. The camera was still rolling, though I had long forgotten it was there. We talked for over an hour without a break.

When the conversation finally ended, it was in the same way it had begun: complete and total bewilderment. Although light had been cast on the situation, Ben and Rhea remained in the dark. They simply couldn't, or wouldn't, understand.

Someone from the *60 Minutes* crew yelled, "That's a wrap!" I got up from the couch and tried hugging my mother-in-law, but she pushed my arms aside and rushed to the bathroom. She stayed there for a long time.

The crew packed their equipment as fast as they had set it up. We signed some sort of legal document giving our permission to air the segment, and agreeing not to hold *60 Minutes* responsible for anything. We were assured it was the usual protocol.

The air was very heavy after the crew left. I heard some chairs being pushed back into their places. Mom came out of the bathroom red-eyed. She invited us to her revived kitchen table for a cup of tea and rugalach. As we sipped the hot tea and munched on the rich pastries filled with butter, cream cheese, cinnamon and raisins, we quietly rehashed many of the points already shared. Warren's parents were traumatized and weary. Nothing could ease their pain and confusion.

"Why did you want to embarrass us on national TV?" Ben asked, not fully meeting our gaze.

"We never wanted to embarrass you," Warren explained. "We wanted to share our struggle. We wanted—"

"It's humiliating," he interrupted. "It's a violation of our privacy."

"Maybe a segment on why people *have* kids would've been more helpful," Warren retorted.

"People have kids because it's normal!" Rhea shrieked. She left the kitchen abruptly, and her husband followed.

I cleared the table, washed the dishes, and joined Warren in the guest bedroom. We held each other in a long embrace. He kissed my eyes tenderly and nuzzled my neck.

"I guess my parents feel we're selfish, huh?" Warren asked.

"And they're truly devastated," I reminded him. "When grandchildren's photos are passed around, they'll have nothing to share."

Although upset by Warren's parents' reactions, we felt that a great weight had been lifted. Finally, we had told the truth. We felt like fearless warriors. There would be no more pats on my belly. No more whispers of, "Go home and practice."

In the morning, I heard the movement of a piece of paper under our door. I got up and read it.

When you were married, we waited to be told

To expect God's gift, more precious than gold.

We wanted to have grandchildren!

We wanted to see your joy in raising a little you and me.

And now we know, there's nothing more to say

You don't want children,

You live only for today!

To whom will you leave all your worldly goods?

To the robbers, the junkies, or just the plain hoods?

But this is how our story ends.

Our children, though married . . .
Are really just friends.

It was signed, "Love, Mom."

The shock of reading that poem was followed closely by a growing need to reach more people. I felt frustrated that, in my in-laws' eyes, no baby for me and Warren equaled no love between us. I shuddered to think how many others who chose not to parent were castigated, or even shunned, by their families. Yet, the poem reflected genuine feelings I couldn't discount. They were worried about our legacy. What mattered to us was what we did here and now; how we led our lives, meaningfully and ethically; and taking responsibility for ourselves, as well as demonstrating compassion for others.

I ran to the phone to reach my own mom, dad and stepfather before my in-laws got to them. I wanted them to know about the *60 Minutes* segment, and be prepared for its airing.

I could see the light at the end of the tunnel. What I didn't anticipate was that it wasn't just any light. It was the train itself coming full force and aimed right at me.

4

Reverberations

We breathed easier after telling my in-laws the truth: they finally knew we weren't going to have children. It was as if pounds of worry and frustration had fallen away.

We felt genuinely sorry for Ben and Rhea. They wholeheartedly believed that grandchildren were the rewards of parenting. They longed for the experience. They wanted to spoil our child, teach him about his ancestors, share family traditions, have sleepovers and play games. Not only had we failed to fulfill those expectations, now they knew we never would. Although I empathized, I knew our choices had to reflect our needs, not theirs.

The decision aside, we felt derelict in sharing a deeply private moment with millions of *60 Minutes* viewers. What were we thinking? In the aftermath of the taping, I almost wished we *were* drug addicts, as Rhea had momentarily suspected. At least then we would have had an excuse to broadcast our personal life across the nation: We had suffered a drug-induced moment of depraved indifference.

A few months later, our segment, "Three's a Crowd," aired on Mother's Day. Sitting in front of my mom's TV with Mom, Sam and Warren, I felt both excited and nervous. I wasn't sure what to expect. If the few minutes that followed didn't teach me to expect the unexpected, I don't know what will.

A clip from *Tea for Two*—that 1950s black-and-white movie with Doris Day and Gordon MacRae—appeared on the screen. A young man and woman were seen gazing into each other's eyes. "We will raise a family," the young man sang, "a boy for you, a girl for me. Can't you see how happy we will be?" The movie faded and Mike Wallace began to speak.

"Good evening everyone," he began. "Recently, more and more couples are choosing not to raise a family. Let's join Warren and Marcia from Long Island, New York, speaking with Warren's parents about that choice. Is this couple smart, or simply selfish? Watch, then decide for yourself."

There was Warren, looking bored and expressionless. His head turned from right to left, right to left, from me to his parents, like a bobblehead doll on a dashboard. As the camera panned to focus on my face, I wished I had washed my hair the night before.

My in-laws sat with furrowed brows. My father-in-law puffed away on his cigar; my mother-in-law sat at attention, leaning slightly forward, rigid. When they spoke, they didn't sound like themselves; their voices were thick with pain and hurt.

I felt like screaming, but I couldn't breathe. And the more I watched, the more upset I became.

Several hours of film had been cut to three minutes of pure propaganda. Our heartfelt conversation had been edited to death, mutilated. Nothing about my passion for teaching, or fondness of children, and nothing at all from Warren; not one word he had said ended up on tape. The time devoted to other childfree couples was even worse. They appeared selfish and insensitive, flaunting their material wealth and hedonistic pleasures. One couple waved from their yacht; another from the cockpit of their private plane. Our commentary on the positive aspects of parenting was nowhere to be seen. Our discussion of the many joys associated with that lifestyle, joys we would miss, had been omitted. The purpose of the segment as we understood it—to speak the truth about the realities of parenting, gain societal acceptance for those who choose not to parent, and raise awareness of N.O.N.—had been lost completely. The immature, ludicrous, featherbrained people who appeared on the screen bore no resemblance to us or the couples we knew. I feared that we had actually done damage to the cause. Now, the entire country would jump for joy that these despicable people wouldn't have children, and their preconceived notions about the childfree would be confirmed.

The show ended with a lovely photo of a mom, dad, and an adorable Gerber Baby look-alike. "My Blue Heaven" played in the background: "Just Molly and me, and baby makes three. We're happy in my blue heaven." The screen faded to black, and Mike Wallace appeared once again.

"Pardon our perversion for showing this on Mother's Day," he said, wearing an expression of intense concern. "Good night, everyone."

We sat there stunned, bewildered, and embarrassed. Nobody spoke for some time. I looked from my mother to my stepfather and back again. Sam wouldn't meet my gaze. He appeared to be transfixed by his hands in his lap. Finally, Mom broke the silence.

"Well, now it's out in the open," she said with a sigh, in that barely audible way with which I had become so familiar. My heart sank. "If that's what you wanted, you got it."

I tried to explain, but she had already excused herself to set the table for dinner. I longed for Sam to laugh—it was my favorite thing about him, that full guffaw—but of course he didn't. He simply placed his large hand on my shoulder and joined my mother in the kitchen.

The next day, I tried to reach Marion Golden. It took several attempts, as her secretary told me, time and time again, that she was either in a meeting or speaking on another line. After countless attempts, I finally got her on the phone.

"I'm shocked," I said. "So much was left out!"

"I'm sorry you feel that way," she answered. "We thought we did a good job."

When I threatened to sue for defamation of character, she responded slowly and deliberately. "You signed a release. You have no case."

The phone clicked off.

I opened my eyes at 8:00 a.m. the following morning. The usual 6:00 a.m. substitute request call hadn't come. It was a surprise. I was a popular substitute, and usually worked every day. I tossed it off as a fluke, and tried to enjoy this unexpected day off. But after a full week of silence where wake-up calls should have been, I became concerned.

"Do you think the show had anything to do with my not working this week?" I asked Warren Saturday morning while sipping my coffee.

"I hate to think it's possible," he said. "It could be a coincidence. Maybe none of the teachers were sick this week."

"Are you saying that to appease me or you?" I replied, walking away.

The lack of work would affect our ability to keep up with bills but, even more than that, I loved my job. I couldn't bear the thought that I might have done something to jeopardize that. I stood looking out our living room window. It was a cold, dreary spring day. The steady splattering of rain against the window-pane was a comfort, as if nature were crying along with me.

Monday morning came and went; still, no phone call. I rallied my courage, and dialed the head of substitute teaching. I asked her why I hadn't been called in, six days in a row. Her answer was curt and blunt.

"Your not working here is a NON-concern of mine," she said before slamming the receiver in my ear.

That confirmed it: the national exposure on *60 Minutes* had resulted in the death of my teaching career. Her reference to N.O.N. couldn't have been clearer. She had either seen the show, or had been told not to hire me.

I asked my best friend Jane what she thought.

"Look, Marsh. People think if you don't want kids, you hate kids. It's like the whole gay thing. If a teacher is gay, they're afraid their kids will turn gay. It's ignorant, but people believe it. That's what society has taught them."

I winced at this revelation. I adored teaching. At the end of a school day, I would stay to write letters to the teachers making sure they knew what topics I had covered. Sometimes, if I had concerns about a child, I called the parents. Or, if a child was wonderful and helpful, I wanted the parents to know about that too. If I taught more than a day or two for one class, I would stop at the library to find books supporting the teacher's lesson plans. I welcomed this as part of my job even though I never got paid overtime. I had the freedom to go above and beyond in this way precisely because I didn't have to rush home to take care of my own children.

What would I do if I wasn't teaching? I didn't know how to type. I was unfamiliar with business. The thought of sitting in an office all day made my skin crawl.

"Maybe I should practice saying, 'Would you like fries with that?'" I said to Jane.

As it turned out, a career in fast food wasn't necessary. Soon after this troubling conversation with my friend, I was asked to appear as a guest speaker at a nearby high school. I had never taught in that school district, but learned that they had a Home and Careers Department interested in presenting my choice because of the alarming increase in teen pregnancies. The hope was that these teens would hear the realities of parenting rather than the romantic fluff they were usually bombarded with, and choose to be more careful when they became sexually active.

I would be paid. We needed the income. It was, at least, a form of teaching. I took the job. I wasn't prepared for what happened next.

As I approached the school building, I saw a group of people walking in what appeared to be a picket line. Some held signs, others beat their fists in the air, as they walked around and around in a large circle. If it was a union line, I decided, I wouldn't cross it. I knew how difficult it was for teachers to get a pay increase. In that moment, I felt for these people, but as I got closer and the signs came into focus, my feelings changed: "Keep Child-Haters Away"; "The Devil's Sister is Speaking Today"; "Children are a Blessing"; "Parents Teach Morality, Strangers Teach Nothing."

A policeman came towards me. "Do you want to enter this building?" he asked.

"Yes," I answered. Truth be told, I had my doubts.

He led me past the marching crowd. They didn't know I was "the devil's sister" herself, and we entered without incident. In the lobby, the principal met me and apologized for the commotion.

"I'm shocked," he admitted. "I never imagined these parents would be so angry."

The speaking engagement went well. The students had tons of questions and seemed to enjoy asking them. I never said I hated kids because, of course, I didn't. I never told them they shouldn't have kids; I didn't feel that way. I simply opened their minds to the realities of parenting—harsh realities which, in recent years, are tossed off as comedy on television shows like "Up All Night," "I Hate My Teenage Daughter," "Raising Hope" and others, but that's a conversation for another time. Could they afford kids? Would they mind giving up their social lives, sleeping late on the weekends, or putting off their plans for college? Were they trained in the proper care of children? Were they prepared for the awesome responsibility of guarding another human being's life? Was this the right time for the career of parenting? The students had never thought of parenting as a career, and were grateful for the fresh perspective. The lecture ended with a humorous exchange between a young man and another student.

"But I want my name handed down!" he challenged.

"Don't worry," a peer called out, "your name is Smith!"

After such a serious conversation, it felt good to laugh.

I stepped aside and waited for the presiding teacher to deliver her closing remarks. She had, for the entirety of my presentation, sat on stage with her hands folded defiantly across her chest. Now she stood and claimed the microphone.

"Thank you for being here," she said coolly, nodding in my direction. She continued, addressing the audience.

"I agree there's a time and a place for having a child. However, if I had known this woman was going to speak to you, I would've blocked her at the door with my body."

The startled students gasped, stiffened, then fell silent. All eyes were on me.

"Of course it would be foolish to have children at your age. However, when the time is right, I hope you don't miss that wonderful experience. I know I haven't."

Some of her students cheered her. Most sat there with their mouths open.

She turned to me once again. "It's all well and good now, not having kids. How will you feel when you're old and alone with no one to take care of you? How will you feel without a grandchild to give you chocolate kisses?"

I had heard that expression before. It's a kiss from the candy-covered face of a child.

"You're a sad excuse for a woman," she told me, and I could tell by the conviction in her voice and the ice in her eyes, she meant it.

The bell rang, and the students made a mad dash for their next classes. I heard animated conversations as the group filed out. Some defended their teacher; others defended me. At first, I was stunned and hurt, fighting back tears of frustration. Then I was pissed! I had reached these impressionable teens, I knew I had. I had hoped they would take a hard look at the facts of parenting, and postpone that choice until they were emotionally ready, financially secure, educated and experienced. That teacher, in one fell swoop, had managed to negate the progress I had made and trivialize the message I had sent.

I left the auditorium feeling dejected and out of sorts. On the way to my car, a teacher who had sat in on the lecture approached me.

"We've already had three pregnancies this semester," she said. "Keep doing this." Then she hugged me.

5

Pronatalism

In a few days, I was over the embarrassment of that hostile teacher. I had taught, which always gave me a great sense of accomplishment, and I was sure I had reached some of the kids, despite the unwelcome conclusion. I had made money too. All in all, the experience was exhilarating.

That same week, I was pleased to receive a letter from a different school district requesting my services as a guest speaker. These requests, over the next year or so, would continue to mount. That particular day, there was another envelope waiting for me with no return address.

"I'm a neighbor," the letter began. "I live in your community. I saw you and your poor husband on *60 Minutes*. I'm disgusted to learn you're a Godless, baby-hating bitch. You obviously lack real love for your husband. Wouldn't you want to bear a child in the likeness of him? Why announce you don't to the world? You've reduced holy matrimony to sleeping together. You should not call yourself a woman because it's unnatural for any woman not to want kids. If I were you, I would be careful about your dog. She's obviously taking the place of a baby. You may find her dead one day."

My hands shook as I called Buffy inside, pulled down the blinds, and locked the doors.

That evening, I told Warren about the threatening letter.

"Marsh, maybe you should stop speaking," he suggested.

"Like hell I will!"

The hate mail kept coming, as did negative reactions from friends and family regarding my choice, but the backlash only fed my determination to speak the truth about parenting: It's a choice, not an inevitability. Pronatalism—a concept to which I had first been introduced via Peck's second book, *Pronatalism: The Myth of Mom & Apple Pie*—took hold of my consciousness, and didn't let go.

Pronatalism is just what it sounds like: pro-birth. It's the dangerous assumption, supported by our society through advertising, pop culture, and by extension, cultural morals, that all women will procreate; the expectation that all women *want to* procreate. It glorifies parenthood by discounting the realities of raising children. It ignores the frightening news stories we see every day about postpartum psychosis, child abuse, and runaways. It denies the alarming number of teenagers and adults who are, for a variety of reasons, ill-equipped to parent. Worst of all, it robs all of us—both women and men, although men are rarely mentioned—of our free will.

In the wake of our *60 Minutes* segment, I experienced a burning desire to identify examples of pronatalism in everyday life. What I discovered confirmed Peck's thesis: Pronatalism is all around us.

I had never realized the way children are used to depict normalcy until I started to monitor TV ads. In the past, I had lowered the sound of bellowing ads which urged us to buy this product or get that service, using that time to find a snack, or take a trip to the bathroom. Now I stood on guard, my pronatalism antenna poised and ready.

One evening soon after, I was preparing dinner, the TV chattering in the background. Then I heard it.

"Warren!" I yelled, running from the kitchen into the living room. "I just heard my first pronatal ad!"

He stopped tinkering on his guitar, and gave me his full attention.

"It's an ad for Campbell's Soup," I explained eagerly. "It ended: 'It's not soup till mother makes it.' If that's true, what the hell did I make for lunch yesterday?"

"Marsh, they're trying to equate their soup with the homemade stuff, mostly made by moms," Warren said, trying to talk me down. "They want to sell soup. That's all."

"I know, but they're selling more than soup," I pleaded. "They're selling the scene too, the old mom-and-apple-pie myth. Moms stay home and cook for their families. That's love. That's the *only* kind of love. But men make their soup, and childfree women make their soup."

I was onto something.

I wrote a letter to The Campbell Soup Company sharing my concerns about the presence of pronatalism in their advertising. Surely, they weren't marketing to mothers and mothers only. I suggested that, in future ads, they consider depicting a more varied and realistic sampling of consumers.

They responded a few weeks later with a case of Campbell's tomato soup and a note: "We thank you for taking the time to write. We appreciate your thoughts and hope you will continue to use our products."

The ad, of course, continued to run.

In that same year, 1974, I heard my first pronatal song. Paul Anka's "You're Having My Baby" wafted over the radio. He and his partner sang:

[Paul]
Having my baby,

What a wonderful way to say how much you love me.

Having my baby,

What a lovely way of saying what you're thinking of me.

[Odia Coates]

I'm a woman in love and I love what it's doing to me.

I immediately saw dangers in the lyrics of this song. First of all, it wasn't his baby; it was theirs. Secondly, when you're fifteen years old, or you don't have the skills, money, or patience to parent, the only thing you're "saying" by having a baby is that you make poor decisions. And what about those who want children but can't have them, how were they affected by this song?

I thought about my friend and her husband who suffered miscarriage after miscarriage. They finally came to terms with the fact that children would simply not be a part of their lives. They were disappointed, of course, but they found other ways in which to prove their love and devotion to one another. When he got sick, she was there for him. When she lost her job, he helped her regain the confidence necessary to find another. She became a devoted aunt, and he a devoted uncle. They both volunteered at a local Boys and Girls Club.

I thought about the teens I encountered at the various high schools at which I spoke. I wondered how many impressionable girls would use pregnancy to bind their boyfriends to them; these girls had, after all, proved their love by having "his" baby.

"You're Having My Baby" may have been the worst pronatal offender in 1974. That song remained number one for a long time. Every time I heard it, I wanted to gag. There hasn't been a song since then that ruffled my feathers the way that one did.

There were, however, other troublesome tunes. "Butterfly Kisses" by Bob Carlisle and Randy Thomas, for example, hit the top of the charts in the '90s. The song was written for one of their daughter's 16th birthday. It paints a warm picture of daddy's little girl growing up before his eyes, and the many Kodak moments they shared. Along the way, she gives him butterfly kisses—when you blink your eyelashes against another's cheek. Carlisle shares his fond memories and reflects, "In all that I've done wrong, I know I must have done something right/To deserve a hug every morning and butterfly kisses at night."

Without a doubt, it's a sweet, tender song. It's also pronatal. Sure, there are fathers who relate to this song, but there are also many who may never know that feeling: fathers who, for one reason or another, lack that special connection with their daughters. The listener's natural tendency to focus on the romantic myths of fatherhood, rather than the conspicuously absent realities, creates a yearning to experience those often impossible Kodak moments. The expectations of fatherhood (or motherhood, of course)—butterfly kisses and birthday parties and an unbreakable bond—don't always match the realities. But no one wants to sing about that.

In fact, I've never heard even one realistic song about having children. When I Googled "negative songs about having children," the following "related" searches popped up: songs about babies, songs about having a baby, songs about pregnancy, songs about family, songs about sons, songs about daughters. All of the songs listed were overwhelmingly positive.

So no one has (yet) had the courage to croon about the nitty-gritty of parenting: the heightened stress levels, lack of sleep, decline in sexuality, or the enormous financial responsibilities, to name a few. I wondered if anyone would write a song about the realities being raised by people who weren't ready or hadn't wanted to parent.

Eminem's "Cleaning Out My Closet" caused a shockwave in 2002 when it was released. He dared to claim that his mom had neglected and mistreated him, a public statement which challenged our society's deep-seated and incredibly misguided belief that all mothers are good mothers. The phrase "cleaning out my closet" refers to Eminem's attempt to reveal the truth about his experience. Despite the fact his mother's perspective is absent, it's safe to assume that they both had tremendous difficulties with the mother-son relationship that neither of them had expected, or desired.

Crystal Bowersox, runner-up in 2010's *American Idol*, recently released "Farmer's Daughter," an emotionally raw song about her abuse at the hands of her mother.

In a recent interview on *The Ellen DeGeneres Show*, Crystal admitted her song was risky and a bit heavy. However, it spoke the truth. Her mom was single, taking care of three kids, with little money or emotional support; she couldn't handle it. She took to drinking when the usual frustrations of parenting set in. The result was physical abuse of her children: "You'd come home with bourbon breath, Jack in the air/And when you broke my bones, I told the school I fell down the stairs."

The media reaction has been positive; the audience's reaction, sympathetic. Many abused children connect to the song's lyrics. This is one of the first musical compositions which dares to suggest that not all moms are ready, willing, or able to parent. I'm pleased to say that pronatalism, as ubiquitous as it is, has no place here. Although the fact that "Farmer's Daughter" never made it big like "You're Having My Baby" may be read as a comment on the messages our society chooses to embrace or ignore.

As I write this, the holiday season is upon us. Publix, a large grocery chain in the South, aired its new holiday ad, depicting a family exchanging hugs and love while women scurry about preparing a festive meal.

"At this time of year," the voiceover chimes in, "let's remember the important things in life." Close-up of the happy family and many children counting their blessings around the dinner table.

Of course, Publix wants to sell food, but the scene also sells the idea that all families live together in warmth and harmony. For those who lack family or close ties, there's sadness. Those who do gather are made to feel inadequate for failing to live up to this impossible ideal. Tensions exist, emotions run high, and disappointments arise when children choose not to visit. That's the reality. Finally, those deciding whether or not they want children are confronted with yet another idealized, unrealistic portrait of family life. Naturally, you see it, and you want it. The problem is the staggering amount of people who won't have it, but they won't know that until it's too late.

Holiday air time could be much better spent. Rather than distracting viewers with pronatal propaganda, supermarket chains might take the opportunity to suggest that we embrace the season of giving. They could encourage viewers to think about homeless people, hungry families, abandoned or abused children, and ask us to find a cause worth helping.

The question I ask is, does advertising mimic life or does life mimic advertising? Can pronatalism affect people's ability to think rationally about the decision to parent? How can it not when all we see is a skewed vision of the responsibility, bathed in myths and masked by lies? Ads that use children to sell products which have absolutely nothing to do with children send the message that "normal" people parent, and if you don't parent, you're not normal. What is normal anyway?

I recently tore out a magazine ad for Centerline Homes. "Who Says You Can't Have It All?" the headline screams. The photo shows a family of four people: mom, dad, young son, and daughter, arms wrapped around each other, all bearing intense smiles. Beside this photo are two additional pictures of lavish homes, $750,000 or more. The ad aims to sell expensive homes, that's a given. And yes, people do live in homes. However, how many couples with two children under the age of six can afford homes like these? Subliminally, they're selling another idea:

"having it all" means having children. You are empty, deprived, and unfulfilled without them.

I've felt pronatalism in restaurants. I object to special kids' meals. Now, don't get angry with me. I know they eat less, and it's a waste to serve a child a regular-sized portion they'll never finish. But here's the rub: kids' meals cost less. Parents have the opportunity to save money and avoid waste, why can't I? (And tax breaks for parents versus non-parents? Don't even get me started.) What about the rest of us? What about teens, college students, or unemployed people with limited funds? Parents, in this situation (and many others), are given an unfair advantage. By extension, non-parents are punished.

On a recent trip to the west coast of Florida, my husband and I stayed at a well-known hotel chain. We were badly in need of relaxation, and looked forward to a quiet day at the pool. Fat chance! It was teeming with screaming children, doing what kids do: splashing, laughing, kicking, and playing. We tried the beach. Again, there were kids everywhere, throwing Frisbees, shouting as they jumped into the waves, rolling in the sand, making their grand forts and sand castles. It wasn't the activities we objected to; those are the joys of being a kid. We did, however, object to the fact that there was no place for us, no space without children.

We went out for an intimate dinner that night. At the table next to ours, a baby was screaming. When I asked our waiter if we could move to a childfree area, his reaction was one of disgust.

"Madam," he hissed, "we are *not* against kids."

"Neither are we," I replied. "We simply want a peaceful dinner."

Before the no-smoking laws took effect, many restaurants offered smoke-free sections. I sometimes wish we had child-free sections.

Once, Warren and I were at a restaurant celebrating our wedding anniversary. Next to us sat a couple with a little boy, who began squirming and fussing to get out of his seat. His parents allowed him to wander around the restaurant, approaching tables as he saw fit. Most people pinched his cheeks, or engaged him in conversation. Then he chose us. Sure, he was cute chattering away, but we didn't want to talk with him. We were celebrating, and we were hungry. We wanted to eat our baked clams which were getting cold.

"He's adorable," I leaned over and told his mother, who smiled. "I wonder if you would mind taking him back so we can enjoy our appetizer," I asked, smiling back.

Instantly, her smile changed to a scowl. "I guess you have no kids," she said, grabbing the little darling as he started to wail. When she and her husband left, she mumbled something impolite under her breath.

We enjoyed the rest of our meal, relishing the peace.

I recently came across a horrific viral video of a woman standing on a train platform with a baby carriage. She lifts her hand and the carriage rolls away, landing directly in front of a moving train. Watching that video, my heart was in my mouth, yet Matt Lauer on *The Today Show* stated that, as a parent, he was horrified to view that scene. That's what he said: "as a parent." So only parents can sympathize? Who wouldn't feel terror watching that scene? Who wouldn't feel relieved to learn the baby was okay? Childless people, apparently. I'm sure Matt meant no harm, but his is precisely the kind of unconscious statement that perpetuates the problem by exalting the status of parents and discounting the feelings of those who have not raised children.

I used to be an avid fan of Dr. Phil. When a person comes to him for advice, he gets right to the point without any deep Freudian analysis of an oral-anal stage of development. He shoots right from the hip and holds nothing back. He offers suggestions on how to face life's challenges in a healthy way.

During a recent episode I was enjoying, he said, "Okay, gather your kids around. Coming up, a new character on Sesame Street I want you to meet. His name is Dr. Feel!"

I looked around me. There were no kids.

By all means, Dr. Phil, invite the children in the audience to meet that new character, but do it without pronatalistic assumptions. He could have said, "If you have kids around, gather them up." That at least would have sent the message that having kids in your home is a choice, rather than a destiny.

I recently responded to a letter to the editor in Florida's *Palm Beach Post*. The letter was written by a man, in response to gay marriage. He wrote, "Marriage is a union that results in the propagation of mankind. Marriage has a special meaning. It does not stand for only a union; it defines an obligation to the future."

I saw red, and responded with the following:

"It's a shame people still are misled by the dangerous belief that marriage must result in procreation. Did the writer of Sunday's letter, 'Gays entitled to rights but not to use the word marriage,' take a fertility test before he married to see whether they could have a child? Should that now be the prerequisite for getting married?

"The obligation for marriage now, or in the future, is not just to procreate. There are many who can't, shouldn't, or simply don't want to. In my opinion, the reason for marriage is love."

Pronatalism is pervasive in our culture, from advertising to entertainment to social interaction, and it's dangerous. It perpetuates myths. It influences people to view the career of parenting through rose-colored glasses. It excludes non-parents from the cult of normalcy. It bathes one of the most important choices you'll ever make in false hopes and unrealistic expectations. Worse, it makes that decision for you.

Childless people are believed to have less in life. In reality, they may have more.

6

Childless vs. Childfree

Once you become aware of pronatalism, its song reverberates. The refrain instills fear. It goes something like this: If you never have kids, you'll miss out on life. You should have children. You must have children. If you don't, you are a misfit. Your womb will be barren. Why flout nature? You can have it all! Happiness is just a baby away! If you're infertile, not to worry. In-vitro fertilization, surrogate pregnancy, or adoption will make your dreams come true. Besides, you can't compete socially without the title of "Mom." You'll be missing too much. Hurry! Hurry! That clock is ticking!

For men, children are a sign of maturity, commitment, and virility. They can't wait to make the announcement that they've hit the target, that their sperm are alive and well.

"Did you see his penis?" a new father might say, passing out the cigars. "It's already larger than normal. Just like his dad!"

The decision not to procreate is met with suspicion; it's still considered the alternative lifestyle, alternative to the "normalcy" of fatherhood.

At a wedding I attended recently, the groom claimed the microphone to thank everyone for coming. The wedding occurred three months earlier than originally planned in order to accommodate the bride's family who traveled from Colombia.

"I know you're wondering why our wedding date changed," he said. His young face was flushed with the joy of the day and too many drinks. "No, she's not pregnant! But manana . . .yo no se!"

The guests hooted, hollered, and cheered loudly. Men slapped the groom on the back. Women planted kisses on his cheeks and fought back tears.

"I'll drink to that! Tomorrow's not soon enough for me," his mother shouted, jumping up-and-down and spilling the drink she held in her hand. This led to even more yelling, laughing, and encouragement for the father-to-be.

I had spoken with the bride a few days before. Her brother had flown in from California with his six-year-old son, her ring bearer. She adored her nephew and had been looking forward to spending time with him. But after caring for him for an entire week, rather than a few hours as she had in the past, reality hit hard. Although they shared many lovely moments, the boy's never-ending needs blew her away. For one week, she attended to his temper tantrums, dealt with his picky eating habits, and went to war over bath time. She bent over backwards to entertain him, but those dreaded words—"I'm bored"—kept cropping up. The experience led her to an epiphany.

"Oh my God, Marcia," she said. "Now I know why you didn't have kids. It's one thing playing with them, but 24/7?"

She and her fiancé had a long conversation in which they discovered that they shared many of the same feelings regarding children. He had been having doubts for a while, but had feared telling her. Now the truth was out, and their lives would be better for it. They agreed they wanted to travel and focus on their careers. Children were not on their path in life and perhaps never would be.

That was their decision and their right. Yet, this man had lied publicly, feeling compelled to say what he knew friends and family wanted to hear. After all, he was a man. Men are supposed to want children. Imagine the reaction if he had said, "I know you're wondering why our wedding date changed. No, she's not pregnant! We want to remain childfree." They would have been castigated, challenged, dismissed as strange and selfish.

The sad truth is those without children may have difficulty finding a place in our pronatalistic society. You may be made to feel childless, either by internal or external forces. In reality, you're childfree.

Visiting a new mommy at the hospital, I would often question whether it wasn't too late to have a baby of my own. The room is filled with the joy of birth. Flowers and balloons are everywhere. Gifts abound. The mother and father gaze adoringly into their child's familiar face. Family and friends come in and out, oohing and ahhing at the sight of that precious new life. And who can resist the simple sweetness of a helpless child in the arms of adoring people? Her little head rests on your chest while her tiny hand latches on to your finger.

I confess, those times were difficult for me. My childlessness roared like a wild lion. I wanted one of those! I wanted a child suckling my breast. I wanted to look into the eyes of my own baby, and see myself and the man I love. I wanted that attention too. Every time I've visited new mothers and their precious newborn babies, I felt childless.

Watching my friends name their babies, I felt guilty. At every bris, the rabbi would sing his blessings and announce the Hebrew name bestowed upon the child. Often the name was chosen in honor of a deceased relative. The family would dab at their teary eyes, relieved that the circle of life remained unbroken: That relative's legacy would live on through the child, the new addition to the family. At these times, I was confronted with the painful fact that my grandparents' names would not be passed on. There would be millions of Harrys or Roses, but not my Grandpa Harry or Grandma Rose. I felt childless at baby naming ceremonies.

When my father gave me a handwritten family tree, I flinched. The names of my grandfather's sisters and brother from Russia called out to me: Bella, Rachel, Sonya, Natasha, and Tevya. Their spirits reached me, although I never knew them. Many times I wondered who they were and what their lives were like. They hadn't had time to have children because they had been exterminated in the Holocaust. With that knowledge came an overwhelming sense of failure. I had failed to produce children who would carry on these dear relatives' names, and ensure that they are never forgotten.

I scanned the rest of the tree, the branches heavy with off-spring. My own branch, of course, was bare. It stood alone, sad and empty, next to my cousins' which bore the branches of their many children below. The children's names taunted me. Other than the people exterminated—those who didn't have a choice—my branch was the only one that hadn't flowered. As a Jewish woman, alone in her decision, I felt embarrassingly childless.

At friends' houses, I experienced a moment of loss upon seeing plaster of Paris molds of their children's little hands standing on a bookshelf. Confronting their kids' art, writing, or report cards proudly displayed on refrigerator doors, I felt a pang in my gut. My refrigerator door was blank white, barren. I felt childless.

All those firsts—first word, first step, first sentence, first tooth, first day of school, first kiss, first prom, and first graduation—would never be a part of my life. Each time I heard about or attended one of those first events, I confess I felt childless.

When my good friend Linda's son Steven sang his Haftorah at his Bar Mitzvah, I sighed. I would never know that magical moment for myself, never witness my son come into manhood and take on the responsibilities of his religion. It's a sweet, sweet moment that I will never have. It's a gift that I won't give my family.

At numerous family weddings, I felt a stab of pain upon witnessing the parents escort their child down the aisle. I realized I would never know that awesome moment, and my child-lessness reared its ugly head once more.

At high school reunions, among peers sharing pictures of their children and, in later years, grandchildren, I felt different, hopelessly "other," excluded from the "normal" progression of life's expectations and rewards. I was self-conscious, afraid that my peers considered me an outsider and a failure. It seemed that my other accomplishments meant nothing. I suddenly ceased to be Marcia the talented teacher, or loving wife, or productive member of society. I was a childless classmate, and nothing more.

I've often wondered, had I had children, if I would join in the passing of those exalted photos. Probably yes, although I've hated having photos extended to me for my approval. Not because I didn't have photos of children to share. Not because I hadn't joined their parents club. Simply because the exchange is often insincere. Who would ever inspect a photo and say, "Wow, he's not exactly handsome, is he?" or, "Sorry she didn't inherit your good looks"? These pictures, these moments, are dear and sweet to the parents and the parents only.

Okay, I admit it: among excited picture passing, I've felt childless.

At the ballet, theater, art shows, and concerts, I sometimes felt envious watching parents introduce their children to culture. How cute the kids look dressed in their special outfits! The girls have bows in their hair. The boys look tidy, and squirm in their white shirts and pressed pants. I would watch parents bend down and whisper into their children's ears. Maybe they're explaining something? Maybe they're telling them how proud they are because they're behaving so well. I would have loved doing that with my child. At those moments, I've felt childless.

Occasionally, TV shows like *Ellen* or *The Today Show* feature child prodigies who can play the piano like Mozart, dance like Jennifer Lopez, or sing like Nicki Minaj. Coming from a long line of talented actors, musicians, and artists, I naturally assume that my own child would have those abilities. I would have loved watching my child perform, showing off his or her hard-earned talents. Watching other children perform and their parents swell with pride and adoration, I've felt childless.

Time and time again, I've felt childless, less than, incomplete. But the thought process doesn't have to end there. I've come to realize that, within these potentially painful moments, are nuggets of reality that cannot be ignored. There's a way to go back and analyze those moments from a different perspective, one that makes use of intellect rather than pure emotion. Imagine the various moments I've mentioned as snapshots, Kodak moments, the joys of parenthood freeze-framed in the childless person's mind. We know what we see: precious moments we won't experience, satisfactions we'll never have. Now stand back and consider all that we don't see. What happened before those sweet moments? What happened after?

Take that scene in the hospital room after a birth, for example: a heartwarming picture of mother, father, and child. Pure bliss, right? Wrong. Pronatalism blinds us to the reality of the situation.

"Okay, Marcia, you've missed this moment," my cousin Risa said when I admitted that I felt jealous seeing her hold her newborn girl. "You've also missed nine months of puking, pushing hemorrhoids back inside your asshole, watching stretch marks expand, fighting hormonal ups and downs, and blowing up like a balloon." She took a breath, clearly disturbed by those uncomfortable memories, and continued. "Don't forget, that baby takes over your body completely. It's not all sunshine and rainbows."

This is the reality, yet those unappealing snapshots are never shared. When I saw them in my mind's eye, the pronatalistic mystique was shattered. I was no longer childless; I was child-free. It's amazing how four little letters make such a profound difference in the way parenthood is perceived.

Once that bundle of joy arrives at home, a whole new set of challenges surfaces. New mothers and fathers stay awake all night tending to the needs of their child. They become slaves to those primal screams, a constant reminder that their lives are no longer their own. They give themselves over to the life they've created, and say goodbye to the many freedoms they once enjoyed. That realization can be terrifying.

"Yeah, I remember sex, but just barely," a friend told me after admitting that he had his own post-partum reaction after the birth of his son. "There's no spontaneity anymore. Our life revolves around the baby."

Nowadays, more and more men are being open and frank about the negative effects of children on their relationships with their wives. Often, intimacy—both sexual and emotional—takes a dive due to attention the child demands. The child comes first; the marriage second.

"When I see my wife adoring our baby, I have mixed feelings," a friend's son admitted. "I love watching her as a mom, but I'm jealous that I'm now number two."

Reflecting upon the intimate relationship I enjoy with my husband, I'm happy to be childfree.

Now, at baby naming ceremonies, I smile when the baby is named for a person who has passed. Although I can't honor family members by passing on their names, I can leave a legacy in other important ways.

I recently enjoyed a long conversation with a former student of mine. She's conflicted between the Chinese customs her parents expect her to uphold and her new Americanized views. She's torn between the desire to show respect for her parents' beliefs and the acknowledgement of her own wants and needs. She sees an unbridgeable chasm between these two lives. I listened to her concerns and, using a role-playing technique, taught her how to navigate the bumpy road to compromise. At the end of our time together, she told me that she felt a great weight had been lifted. I hadn't passed on a family name, but I had shared wisdom which would affect both hers and her daughter's life for the better. I felt my ancestors smiling down in approval. They had helped others during their lives, and now I was too. That legacy is just as important as a name, if not more so. I'm childfree, yet still manage to honor my ancestors and contribute positively to others' lives.

I've reached countless children as teacher, aunt, friend, and neighbor. Those names don't belong on my family tree; they're not part of my biological family. Still, I hold them close with as much love and devotion as if they came from my own body. Yes, my branch stands alone, but that's only on paper. I have many children in my heart.

Now, when parents share photos of their children, I chuckle to myself. Those photos capture only the happy moments. Where are the photos of the child's temper tantrums, or that time he said "I hate you"? Where are the pictures of the sick days? How about the turbulent teenage years? You never see a photo of the argument that ensued when a teenager came home late, or the hours of racing hearts and floor-pacing that came before. Think of all those unpleasant moments inherent in raising children that we'll never see. When I remind myself of the reality, I am definitely childfree.

Even those exciting firsts, as appealing as they sound, come with a price. Take the first day of school, for example. The experience is bittersweet. On the one hand, there's the satisfaction of seeing your child take the first step towards independence, putting on a brave face as she climbs onto the bus, lips quivering, waving a tentative goodbye. On the other hand, there's the inevitable separation anxiety, the difficult adjustment to an empty home for most of the day, every day. Thinking about all the hard work and devotion necessary to be a good parent, only to send your child away first to school and then off into life without you,

I breathe a sigh of relief that I'm childfree. I fear the pain of disconnection would kill me.

And yet, there's another piece to this puzzle that's not often shared. I remember watching mothers from my window on the first day of school, waiting for the bus to arrive. Many cried openly, blowing kisses as the bus rounded the corner and out of sight. Then the smiles and champagne glasses appeared, accompanied by exuberant shouts of "Freedom! At last!" Few parents are brave enough to admit that, while their children are at school, they revel in the joys of being childfree.

Of course, they're not childfree, not in the way that I am. Their various responsibilities loom. They're always on call in case of illness or behavioral problems. They must make time to help with homework, or attend parent-teacher meetings. Some have to deal with the added stress of raising a child with ADHD, or dyslexia, or more serious disorders. Some struggle to protect their children from bullying, or other social complications, like not fitting in with the A-crowd. I've seen my own niece's and nephew's hearts crushed when they weren't invited to a child's birthday party. The difficult job of reconstructing a child's self-esteem falls to the parents. When I consider such awesome responsibilities, I celebrate being childfree.

True, I'll never get to hear the adorable story of my child's first kiss. I'll also never have to worry about how that kiss can lead to more kisses and, eventually, sex. It's more than experimentation today. It's sexually transmitted diseases, drugs and alcohol at parties, and sexual experiences at frighteningly early ages. Would I have the courage to teach my own child about the dangers and joys of sex? Would I be able to handle a horrible situation if it came my way? Would I have the strength to support her in the aftermath of a poor decision? Many parents can't. In imagining all that could be, I'm grateful to be childfree.

I watched with pride as my niece got her degree in business. I stood beside my sister and brother-in-law as they snapped countless photographs of their daughter walking across the stage and shaking the university president's hand. What an accomplishment for all of them! I sighed and felt a stab of regret. I would never know this meaningful moment for my own child. Suddenly, my childless snapshot became a childfree reality as I thought about the events leading up to this moment and those still to come: the astronomical tuition my niece's parents paid, extra expenses for tutors, incredible anxiety over schoolwork, and, soon, the pressures and challenges in searching for her first job. Not to mention the empty nest syndrome that my sister and her husband endured when their daughter left for college. No doubt about it, being childfree has benefits.

Yes, I'll never know what it's like to see my child Bar or Bat Mitzvah'd, or wedded to a person he or she loves. And I'll never have to fight to ensure that my child is studying his or her Haftorah portion, hearing them whine, "It's too hard!" or, "I hate learning Hebrew! Can't I just have the party?" I'll never have to force myself to accept a future son or daughter-in-law who I might not approve of—remember, my mother got a taste of this when I married Jack. I'll never go broke from financing an extravagant wedding. Studying the before and after snapshots we never see reminds me of my contentedness in remaining childfree.

Perhaps I missed out on taking pride in my child's artistic accomplishments, but perhaps I didn't. Who can say, without hesitation, that their child will show a propensity for the arts just because his or her family did? And who's to say that those kids I see at concerts and plays, dressed to the nines, are actually little angels? How many of those parents bribed or threatened their children to behave themselves before or during the show? These are hypotheticals, of course, but meaningful in that they represent a larger truth: When it comes to children, what you see or expect is not always what you get. For me, the reality bears more weight than the myth. I'm happy to be childfree.

If you were hoping to read a chapter in which you clearly see that being a childfree person is better than being a childless person, I can't give you that. Many times, I've felt the emotional void of childlessness, and I'm sure there will be many more. It helps to reexamine those moments objectively, without the veil of pronatalism coloring my outlook, and consider what it is I'm actually missing. A handful of Kodak moments, yes, but more importantly, a lifestyle that I decided, long ago, simply isn't for me. In the end, perhaps the force that pulls at me is not the desire for motherhood at all. Perhaps it's the desire for acceptance from a pronatalistic society, one which trains me to ask the dangerous question, if you're not a mother, what are you? My answer is simple: childfree.

7
Heart to Heart

There are many ways to have children in your life without raising them. As a teacher for many years, I've made a concerted effort to connect with my students whenever possible. A few of these connections have blossomed into long-term relationships which, to this day, continue to add a rewarding dimension to my life. Of course, from time to time, they've also added worry, pain and frustration. So it is with any worthwhile relationship.

"You know what?" my cousin Risa reflected. "You've been like a mom to those kids."

Like a mom, yes, but not a mom. Not in the true sense of the word. My cherished experiences with these children have been and continue to be part-time. I have the freedom to pick and choose the nature and level of my involvement. Their mothers, on the other hand, have pledged a full-time, never-ending commitment. I haven't taken the place of my students' mothers, nor would I want to. I simply do what I can and leave the rest to family, hoping that I enrich these individuals' lives as much as they enrich mine.

In this chapter, I'll share stories of children I've met, connected with and stayed connected with. If you take nothing else from these anecdotes, please understand that I've pursued and nurtured these relationships, not because I felt a void without biological children of my own, but because these are special people whom I love, despite the fact—or quite possibly because of the fact—that I am not a mother.

From my first day in the classroom at age 22, I've told my students the same thing: "As long as you need me, to the best of my ability, I'll be there for you." I said it and I meant it because I feel strongly that an effective teacher will act as a mentor both in and out of school. Out of the hundreds of children I taught, only a handful actually took advantage of my heartfelt offer. Amy was the first.

She wasn't the smartest little girl in her second grade class. She was an unexceptional student from a blue collar family, living with her mom, dad, brother and sisters in a tract housing project behind the school. Despite her hardships, she had a sparkle in her eye. Her giggle was infectious. When she knew the answer to a question, she would wave her hand frantically to get my attention. She loved pleasing me and would often come to school early to clean the boards or water the plants.

One day, this usually effervescent little girl arrived at our classroom with red, swollen eyes.

"What's wrong?" I asked. "You look sad."

Her lips trembled. "Nothing's wrong," she lied.

I took her hand and asked the same question again, gently lifting her face so that her eyes could meet mine. It wasn't long before the tears poured freely. She wanted to be a Brownie Girl Scout, she told me, but her family couldn't afford the required uniform and dues.

I told her I would try to help. I didn't promise anything but gave her hope. She hugged me and ran to get the sponge to clean the board.

That night, I spoke with her parents who mirrored Amy's story. I asked if they would allow me to pay her bill. They refused. I tried again, explaining that Amy would gain a great deal by becoming a Brownie. Eventually, they accepted my offer with the condition that I join them for dinner no less than once a week as a thank you. Of course, I accepted. I still remember the simple meals of Chung King canned Chinese food and Little Caesar's pizza served on a white plastic tablecloth. Amy would sneak glances at me over the table, obviously proud to have me, her newfound guardian angel, in her home sharing a meal with her family.

The day Amy was sworn into her Brownie troupe, her mother and I stood side by side with tears in our eyes. Amy stood tall in her crisp uniform reciting her oath. She wasn't my child, yet in that moment her mother and I felt the same intense pride.

Although the experience was incredibly fulfilling, I never let myself forget the vast differences between my role and Amy's mother's. I could easily afford the small payments for Amy's Brownie troupe, and didn't need to worry about the family's more significant needs and financial burdens as Amy's mother did. After the ceremony, Amy's mom returned home to her non-stop worries and endless responsibilities that come with having children: medical bills, school work, her son's behavioral issues; the list goes on and on. I, on the other hand, stayed for cookies and punch and went home to prepare my lesson plans, luxuriate in a long bubble bath, and plan a vacation with my girlfriends. Then again, I never got to tuck Amy into bed that night, share a goodnight kiss, or hear her prayers thanking her mom and dad for allowing me to help. Does a long bubble bath trump a goodnight kiss from a child? I'm hard-pressed to think of a more complicated question.

Forty years later, Amy and I are still connected. I've saved a stack of letters documenting her life's journey from school to marriage to starting a family of her own. We've made time to visit each other and shared hundreds of phone calls. I've loved being there for her, listening and suggesting ways to overcome the obstacles she's faced.

I've also suffered with her, helpless to change her mind as she made poor choices. I've felt anguished watching her struggle to raise her own children with little emotional or financial support. I've also endured the heartache of giving her money for a car only to learn that her oldest son totaled it in a drunken rage. As heart-wrenching as these experiences have been, they are nothing compared to what her parents faced. They had to deal, on a daily basis, with the unrelenting drama of Amy's poor choices and now, dysfunctional grandchildren who take much more than they give.

Why do I share this? To refute the perception that all child-free people hate children and suggest that anyone can have a meaningful impact on a child's life without birthing, adopting, or raising that child. My relationship with Amy is testimony to the fact that motherhood is not a prerequisite for love.

॰◌৶

Lan Houng was a student in my first ESL class. When we met, she was in the silent period of language acquisition: the time during which the student struggles with the fear of attempting the new language she seeks to learn. The student often feels unintelligent and as if she doesn't fit into the new culture and its customs. She also wrestles with the profound loss of her native language as well as cultural and familial roots.

Houng was gorgeous with a slender body and long black hair that cascaded straight down her back. Her peers made fun of her almond-shaped eyes, holding their own eyes at an angle and taunting "ching, ching, ching." Needless to say, children can be cruel. The taunts didn't seem to faze her, although I'm sure it was hurtful. She soon began to feel more at ease in our ESL classroom, opening up once others shared their journeys from their respective homelands to America.

Houng had emigrated from Vietnam two years earlier. Her mother, understanding that Vietnam was too dangerous for her youngest daughter, had sent her over alone to live with her brother in New York. Although Houng's mom didn't have the courage, good health or ability to leave, she wanted her daughter to have a better life. Her dream was to provide Houng with more opportunities and a better education than she herself had.

On a rainy morning, she placed her 12-year-old daughter on a small boat with strangers bound for the Philippines. Houng waved goodbye as the boat left the shore and her beloved mother. On shore, her mom whispered fervent prayers for her daughter's safe voyage. I can't even begin to fathom what her mom felt in that moment. Who among us could?

Houng settled in on the packed boat powered by one motor. After a few days at sea in awful living conditions—frequent sea sickness, scanty food and water, and barely any room to move— the motor failed. They drifted a few more days in a frightening storm with high waves crashing on top of them until they were rescued by a fishing boat and brought to their destination.

"I thought I would die," Houng told me in halted English.

When I asked her to tell me more about that journey, she refused. Obviously the memory pained her. I hate to think of the horrors she encountered at such a young age.

Houng's story touched me. I wanted to protect her and help her in any way I could. I made sure the other teachers knew all she had been through so that they could be sensitive to her needs. I stayed after school to tutor her. I kept an eye out for signs of distress or depression, and encouraged her to share her troubles with me. If I had had children of my own, I couldn't have done that. My lifestyle was such that I had time on my hands, much more than the teachers who ran home after school to tend to their own children.

At Houng's middle school moving-up ceremony, I asked the families waiting to acknowledge their own children to help me praise this special girl whose family couldn't be with her. I requested that Houng be adopted for a few minutes by everyone in that auditorium. When she was presented with her certificate, everyone jumped to their feet, hooting and howling in support. Houng stepped up to the microphone. In a small faltering voice she said, "Thank you. Today I am very happy. And I am very sad to leave this school and my ESL teacher. She is my family. Now you are my family." Then she turned and ran into my arms. There wasn't a dry eye in the crowd and I was no exception.

Houng went on to graduate from a good college, marry her high school sweetheart and start her own successful business. We've stayed in close touch.

Last summer, twenty years after meeting her, I visited her and her husband in Pennsylvania. Pulling up to her beautiful home, I was totally unprepared for what I saw. There in her driveway was a large group of people waving at me! She had invited her family to meet her forever teacher. One by one, they came to me, bowed and thanked me for being there for Houng all these years.

After the greetings, Houng presented me with their baby daughter.

"She's your school grandbaby," she laughed.

Being a school grandmother, I've discovered, is a delicious part-time experience. I can send gifts, enjoy photos, and hear stories about first words and first steps. It's the biological grandmother, not me, who spent the night in the hospital when Houng's daughter awoke with a high fever and started to convulse. I didn't even know about it until she was safe at home and healthy once again. I love this child, but I'm not a grandmother. I slept peacefully while the child's true mother and grandmother paced the floors.

When I speak with Houng, which I do often, it's like a breath of fresh air. Her life's philosophy of being grateful for what she has, cherishing her role as a mother, and supporting her family in Vietnam is inspirational. The knowledge that I contributed in some small way to the development of this wonderful person has been fulfilling beyond my wildest dreams.

ഗ൫

Roberto and Elana are siblings from Venezuela who I had the pleasure—and challenge—of teaching. I met Roberto first. He was a bright boy with some serious behavioral issues, showing defiance to teachers and lashing out against peers. He simply refused to march to the beat of the school's drum. As far as he was concerned, rules were meant to be broken!

"He's damaged goods," his guidance counselor warned me.

But I saw beyond Roberto's bad behavior. I knew that, to get on track, he would need clear boundaries, consistent consequences, and a genuine relationship with a person he could count on. I set out to be that person. It wasn't that I had better instincts than his parents, although Roberto did suffer beatings at home; it was that I had the patience and training to know how to approach Roberto in a healthy way. I knew the value of giving him a reason to shine, praising his efforts, and letting him know, reasonably and rationally, when he disappointed and why. Slowly but surely, Roberto responded to my efforts and his behavior improved. One year after meeting him, he introduced me to his younger sister Elana. She became one of my forever friends.

At our first meeting, Elana stared at me out of the blackest eyes I've ever seen. She held her brother's hand tightly, shy at first and not quite sure how to behave. At that time, she spoke very little English. Her brother told her I was a teacher she could trust. It took some work, and she eventually came out of her shell.

I encouraged all of my students, including Elana, to record their thoughts in a journal as an authentic way of experiencing and practicing English. I assured them that it was safe for them to write about anything and share it with me if they wished.

Unfortunately—or maybe fortunately—Elana's writing revealed that she was hiding a terrible burden: repeated sexual abuse by her mother's boyfriend. I informed our principal who brought in Social Services. Both Roberto and Elana were taken from their homes that very night and placed into foster care. I remained at school with them until 11:00 p.m., holding their hands and comforting them, waiting for the police car to come and take them away.

I was heartsick. I felt that I had done the right thing, but as a result, I was responsible for taking two children from their home and out of their mother's care. My head was spinning, filled with unanswerable questions: Was their mother at fault? Did she even know what her boyfriend had done? What were those children now facing? What would become of them? All those shocking stories I had heard about foster care haunted me. I prayed that Roberto and Elana had been placed in a good home with decent people. And as bad as this time was for me, I couldn't even begin to imagine what the children's mother must have been going through.

The story has a happy ending. Although it took another year, I found the kids in a group home close to where I lived. I was able to host them in my home on weekends and holidays. I watched Elana graduate from high school with honors, get a degree in social work, find a terrific job in a hospital and marry the man of her dreams. I was included in the wedding. I sat next to her mother at the reception. It was the family table.

Roberto has had a hard time of it and is still struggling to find his path. His mother and I speak often, sharing our concerns about this man we both love. Where is he headed? Will he be able to provide for his two children? Although I worry and commiserate, his mother worries more. After all, she's loved him since birth, and has been much more involved in his trials and tribulations than I have. She's taken care of his children when his girlfriend couldn't. She's bailed him out of jail when no one else would. She goes to bed at night with the guilt of having failed to teach her son how to take responsibility for his actions. Yet if she's failed in this regard, so have I. Still, I have hope that Roberto will find the strength to turn his life around.

"I'm trying to find happiness," Roberto wrote to me recently. "Knowing you are here for me is an impact that can't be measured."

∽≪

"Mrs. Davis, please go to the guidance office," I heard over the school's PA system one morning. "You have a new student."

Three weeks before, I had finished the last individualized lesson plans for each of my students. Now a new one! I felt a rush of excitement, followed by a moment of concern over who this mysterious student was, how much English she knew, and whether she would be able to transition into my class and our culture smoothly.

When I entered the office, I saw a young girl sitting quietly beside a serious-looking older man. She held his hand so tightly, her knuckles had turned white.

"Mrs. Davis, this is Mr. Mohammedieh," the guidance counselor said, "and this is his daughter, Mahsa. They're from Iran."

I extended my hand to Mr. Mohammedieh, unsure if this brand of greeting was customary or even acceptable in his culture. He responded with a firm handshake. In broken English, he told me that Mahsa was looking forward to joining my class, and that his son Mahyad would be in the elementary school.

I shifted my attentions to Mahsa who was hiding behind her father's legs, looking pale, frightened, and confused. I knew the look. When I held her hand, I felt it trembling. My heart went out to her. There she was, in a new country and a new school, among strangers who spoke a language she had only heard in passing. I could tell by her pleading expression, she knew her father was about to leave her here. He spoke to her in Persian then, perhaps assuring her that everything would be alright. As he let go of Mahsa's hand, her eyes filled with tears.

I grew to honor and treasure my relationship with this family. Over dinner in their immaculate basement apartment, I learned how they had enjoyed a privileged lifestyle in Iran. Mohammadreza Mohammedieh had owned a factory. His wife Zahra had an advanced degree in mathematics. However, living under an oppressive government and witnessing the steady erosion of human rights—they would receive daily reports of arbitrary killings, imprisonments, and unexplained disappearances of neighbors—these brave parents decided that comfort was less important than their children's freedom. So they came to America, and built a new life. Mohammadreza worked as a laborer in a factory similar to the one he had owned in Iran; Zahra worked as a seamstress. Afterhours and on days off, they both picked up shifts in a fast food restaurant. This was a new life indeed.

As for Mahsa and Mahyad, I'm embarrassed to say that not every teacher welcomed them as openly or readily as they should have. Some didn't welcome them at all. Once, I invited Mahsa's Social Studies teacher to sit on Mahsa's class presentation about her culture and customs.

"No, thank you. Do you know what those Muslims have done to the Jews?" he said snidely.

I taught Mahsa and bonded with her family for three years. In the third year, they were finally able to afford a decent apartment on the third floor of a house across the street from the school. They submitted all the paperwork, thrilled at the prospect of fulfilling this first of many dreams here in America.

When several days had gone by without any word from the owner, they called me wondering why. They had thought it was a done deal.

I had my suspicions. During my lunch break, I called the owner and expressed interest in the apartment. The next day, I met him. He showed me the space, then handed me the rental form.

"It's yours if you want it," he said.

"You mean no one else is interested?"

"Nope," he said, pretending to inspect a windowsill so he wouldn't have to meet my gaze.

"I'll take it," I announced, smiling and batting my eyelashes flirtatiously. "I'll take it for The Mohammadieh Family who already told you they wanted it."

"Who?"

"I think you know."

"Who are you?" he asked, eyeing me suspiciously.

I explained who I was, and why I had done what I had to do.

"What if they're terrorists?" he said. "And you know how dirty those Muslims can be."

"I'm sorry you feel that way," I responded coldly. "I believe that's called prejudice, and you could be sued for it." I began to walk away, then changed my mind. "By the way, where did your parents come from?" I asked.

"Italy. Why?"

"I was just wondering who gave them a chance."

Once The Mohammadiehs were settled in this sunny apartment, I was invited for dinner. They gave me a precious bowl they had brought from Iran. The card read, "It is written in the book that you will always be a part of our hearts."

༄

Helping children seems to be my calling. It's that close, personal connection I enjoy, heart to heart.

"It's so sad, Marcia," well-meaning friends and family members have often said. "You would have made a wonderful mother."

Maybe so, but there's nothing sad about it. Being like a mother is good enough for me.

8

Menopause

On a cold, snowy night my initiation into the strange world of menopause began. This was unknown territory for me. Usually, during winter months I would climb into bed with an electric blanket set on high, wearing a long flannel nightgown and wooly socks. I felt a bit guilty coming to bed looking like a snowwoman, but I had no choice. Suffering with Raynaud's Syndrome, I could never get warm during those freezing nights. Sometimes our beloved dog Buffy would be wedged against me. Picture the scene: Buffy on one side, Jim, my husband of one year, on the other, my legs wrapped tightly around him. (Warren and I had eventually split over his extramarital affair.)

"Get your frozen feet off me!" Jim would scream.

On this particular night, a cold wind howling outside, I experienced an unusual sensation: a wave of warmth rolling from the top of my head to the tip of my toes. I was hot. Too hot. Uncomfortably hot. I kicked the covers away. Jim lifted his head off the pillow and looked at me quizzically.

"Oh my God!" I exclaimed. "I think I'm in menopause!"

Memories of my mother flooded my mind, vivid images of her menopausal suffering. During that time, she always carried a small Chinese fan she would whip out of her purse to get relief from the relentless hot flashes. Her weight slowly increased. Her moods were erratic. Her once smooth skin dried out and cracked. Her hair fell out revealing the pink scalp beneath. When she laughed, she ran to the bathroom to avoid drops of urine escaping her body.

In those days, women didn't talk openly about menopause or the transformation their bodies were undergoing. When they did speak up, they referred to "the changes" in hushed whispers amongst their closest friends. They must have recognized the significance of this profound shift in their lives, but whether they discussed it, I can't say. Menopause signaled the end of baby-making in an era during which most women were stay-at-home moms. And although their children were already grown and leading lives of their own, these women still identified as mothers. They were the caregivers, and their self-esteem centered on the fulfillment of that role: raise the children, support the husband, care for the home. With the children grown, husbands retired, less housework to be done, and now the cessation of the period, that powerful reminder of womanhood, what was left? What would they do now? From where would they draw their value?

Lying in my bed feeling the warmth of the hot flash dissipating, I reached for the covers. I was cold once again, appreciating that feeling for the first time. I turned over and grabbed the pillow under me. My eyes popped open. I couldn't sleep! With Buffy next to me breathing deeply and Jim snoring away, I wondered if mothers today experience the same thoughts and feelings as the women of my mother's generation. I thought of my friends who have children. They hadn't waited at home to greet their kids after school with a freshly baked plate of cookies as my mother's friends had. Most of the women I knew had jobs. Many were single moms. After working all day, they came home to clean the house, cook dinner, care for the pets, and micro-manage their children's extracurricular activities. Considering how different their lives were from the women of the

'50s, I couldn't help but wonder, what did menopause mean for them?

Menopause was a hot topic (pun intended) in the school where I taught. Even so, much of the emotional push-and-pull seemed the same as it was for women of my mother's generation. Women still felt sad knowing they no longer had the option to have another child. The only difference I found was in the women's frank openness about the issue and willingness to share intensely personal information. It was common to hear teachers lamenting their diminished or nonexistent sex drive. Never in a million years would my mother have even dreamed of discussing her libido. And in the workplace? Forget it!

Still hugging my pillow, I lay awake listening to the steady cacophony of snoring from my bedmates. By now, Buffy had joined Jim in a rumbling duet. It didn't matter. It was my contemplations, not the snores, that were keeping me awake. I flipped onto my back and concentrated on the soft sound of snow falling against the window. Terrific! I couldn't sleep and had to drive 36 miles to school in a snow storm. I got out of bed, careful not to disturb the dreamers, crept downstairs, and made myself a cup of tea.

Tapping a spoon on the table, I felt uneasy and confused. I had never wanted children. I had never judged my self-worth on the basis of how many children I did or did not birth. I had never tried to procreate. In fact, I had actively tried *not* to procreate, taking precautions against pregnancy at every turn. I didn't know if I even could carry a baby to term and had never cared to find out. I had never thought about my period in the context of children, had never needed to know exactly when I was ovulating. I didn't need my period, not in the functional way other women do, so why was I feeling sad? It didn't make sense. I wondered if other childfree women felt the same.

The soft tap-tap-tapping of Buffy's paws on the staircase told me she was on her way down. She came into the kitchen and looked at me as if wondering why I was up at this ridiculous hour. I let her out the back door and saw the heavy accumulation of snow. Maybe there would be a snow day! God, I needed one.

Buffy came back a few minutes later with her snout covered in snow. She shook herself off, yawned and settled down next to me. I stared into the teacup thinking about what menopause might mean for me. It signaled the end of my period, of course, a change I welcomed. Finally, I would find relief from the cramps, bloating and diarrhea that had besieged me monthly since age thirteen. My period always seemed to appear just in time for a long-awaited vacation or special event. I would down Midol and curse my body for betraying me. I always felt it was a waste for me to suffer those discomforts. I had chosen not to have children, damn it! Yet month after month, year after year, those unpleasant periods had arrived. Saying goodbye to my periods would not be difficult. Still, I felt a distinct sense of loss. The emotion unnerved me. I could barely bring myself to ask the question that weighed heavily on my mind: Was it possible that, all these years, deep down, I had actually wanted children?

My mind reeling, I dragged myself back upstairs to try to sleep.

৩৩

When the alarm clock rang, I realized I had slept about two hours. After showering, I stood before the full-length bathroom mirror. The heat and moisture from the hot shower made the mirror sweat. I scrutinized my reflection as the fuzzy outline of my body slowly came into focus.

I really hadn't changed much in the past ten years. I had expected to see obvious signs of aging—sagging breasts, wrinkled thighs, or those ugly, flabby underarms—and maybe even some sudden transformation since the night before. I was in menopause, after all! But I saw none of that. I looked pretty good for my age. All those years of exercising and eating right seemed to have paid off, not to mention the stretch marks and cellulite I had avoided by never becoming pregnant. Okay, I admit I saw wrinkled knees. I could live with that. Peering closer, I saw tiny lines on my upper lip, radiating upwards and thickening. My eyelids weren't as tight as they used to be; they were beginning to droop. I noticed a pronounced line of gray at the roots of my hair, and I made a mental note to have it re-dyed.

Then, right then and there, standing naked in the bathroom, I had an ah-ha moment. I realized my sadness over menopause was rooted, not in some dormant desire to have children as I had feared, but in the sudden impossibility of it. Before my first hot flash, I had felt that pregnancy was still a viable choice. I had never wanted to change my mind, but always felt it was an option. Now, it wasn't, simple as that, and it all felt so unbelievably final. The word "end" loomed before me—the end of youth, the end of life, the final word on a decision I had made decades ago—and I was scared.

I didn't know much about this mysterious stage of my life I had entered without warning. I decided that I would find a way to accept these endings as a natural and unavoidable part of life. I would come to terms with the reality, I told myself, in the same way I had, years earlier, accepted that I can't last as long on the dance floor, or sleep through the night without getting up to pee.

Instead of standing in front of my mirror lamenting over breasts that had never fed a baby and never would, I decided to celebrate my life. Wisdom should come with menopause, shouldn't it? Actually, I did feel wiser! Acceptance of aging and the freedom to be and do whatever I wanted gave me strength. Rather than convince myself that my eggs had been wasted, I concentrated on the various ways in which I had created: not literally, but symbolically. By sharing my own life, the lessons I had learned and skills I had mastered, I had and would continue to make others' lives better.

Jim knocked on the bathroom door and entered wearing a huge grin. He had just received a call that school was canceled due to the snow storm. He asked if I wanted to go back to bed or have breakfast with him. I needed to talk and accepted his breakfast invitation. Before long, I could smell bacon, toast and hot coffee wafting from the kitchen.

Over breakfast, I told Jim about my troubled evening and morning, and also shared my revelations: although I was still sure I didn't want children, I was sorry to see the option go; and despite the sudden finality of my choice, I could still act as a creator of life, a mother by behavior if not biology. These conclusions sounded even truer when I spoke them aloud.

Jim listened attentively, then reached across the kitchen table, took my hands in his, and said, "Just want you to know, I'm perfectly happy being a family of two, plus Buffy."

I cried tears of happiness, and told him how much that meant to me.

"By the way," he added, "does menopause mean we don't have to use birth control anymore?" His grin told me he liked that prospect.

ৎৄৄৄ

Over the next few months, I read as much as I could about menopause. I also took part in seminars in order to face the reality head-on. I had a list of questions I needed answered. Were hormonal replacement therapies safe? What about alternative therapies, like the medicinal use of herbs? What could I do about the serial yeast infections that were sure to come? What about the vaginal itching and dryness I had heard so much about? Would intercourse be painful?

I quickly learned that most of the women in those seminars were not after the kind of concrete information that I was. I was seeking education; they were seeking emotional support in dealing with the loss of their baby-making years. Clearly, these mothers were struggling.

"I feel totally useless now," one woman shared. "Having and raising my babies defined me. Who am I now?"

"I know how you feel," another woman responded. "When I see a baby, all I do is cry. I'll never have that again, the chance to hold my baby in my arms. I'm praying for a grandchild, but my daughter only talks about her career."

"I get weepy when I see one of those ads on TV with a woman holding a baby," a third woman added. "It's over for me."

When my time came to speak, I chose my words carefully. I had my own agenda, but didn't want to offend.

"I never had a child," I said.

The group awwwwwed.

"Actually, I chose not to have children."

Now, the group fell silent. Some women raised their eyebrows and made meaningful eye contact with others across the circle. Some stared at me as if I were an alien.

"I'm here to learn how to overcome health challenges during menopause," I continued.

When I tried to tell them that I was happy not to have those unwelcome periods, the majority of them didn't understand. I attempted to explain, but could see that I was getting nowhere. The women were defensive, as if hating my period somehow equated to hating them or worse, all women. Eventually, I stopped trying to explain, sat back and waited for the topic of hormonal replacement therapy to arise.

When it came to the physical demands of menopause, I was lucky. The hot flashes weren't that bad and didn't last long. I fought gaining weight with a vengeance. I started Jazzercising, eating organic foods, and taking more vitamins. To attack the dreaded wrinkles, I added a morning body lotion regimen to my usual nightly routine. I stopped sunbathing and used high SPF sunscreens every day.

Sitting in my gynecologist's office waiting for my annual check-up, the news came on their TV. Usually I tune out those blaring broadcasts, opting instead to page through a magazine. This time, I watched and listened with growing alarm.

"A Russian woman in her 60s is a mother for the first time," an excited newscaster exclaimed. The camera zoomed in on an ecstatic, wrinkled woman holding an adorable, chubby baby.

"I never thought I could have a child at this age," she told the reporter. "I never wanted one. But I recently started doubting that choice, and changed my mind. Thanks to all the medical advances, here's Natasha! To think I might have missed this!"

After this newscast, I started noticing more and more reports of babies being born to older mothers. The media focused on well-known personalities—singers, models, and movie stars—having success with in vitro fertilization and surrogacy. A photo of Celine Dion, her beaming husband and their new baby dressed in an exquisite layette appeared in all the tabloids. Becoming a mother, she announced, was the proudest moment of her life. It was worth all the struggles with infertility. Stories about the late pregnancies of Christie Brinkley and Cheryl Tiegs plastered women's magazines. In 2010, John Travolta's wife Kelly Preston announced that she was pregnant at 47. Joan Lunden openly discussed the fact that her twins had been carried by a surrogate.

I was happy for those women finally enjoying the benefits of motherhood. Who wouldn't be? Really! They had fought a long battle with infertility and won. But I also wrestled with my emotions, feeling annoyed. Here was a new example of pronatalism. As I was in the throes of menopause, struggling to come to terms with its hard realities, the media was undoing all that hard work by pushing on the public unrealistic propaganda. Yes, they were saying, it can still happen for you! Who says you have to allow nature to take its course? Women of the world, make babies … forever! I was amazed at all the vital information the media was guilty of omitting: the enormous expense of in vitro and surrogacy; the personal trainers, private chefs, and plastic surgery that allow these celebrities to look as healthy and well-rested as they do immediately after childbirth; and the emotional hardships that they had surely endured from the countless failed attempts at pregnancy.

I couldn't help but wonder, how many older women would be affected by all the hype surrounding those celebrities? Maybe I do want to have a child of my own, an older woman might think. Maybe it isn't too late after all. To these women, I say follow your heart, but be aware of where your desires are coming from. If having a child at such a late age is a genuine need, then by all means, do what will make you be happy, but do so with the knowledge that nature may not have intended it. Know that serious health risks are involved. Know that you may not be around to see your child graduate from high school. If you are being persuaded to procreate by society, media, or any external, pronatalistic force, I urge you to rethink your motivations. Remember, this important decision is yours and yours alone.

"If you never had children, you'll mourn that loss," one of my seminar leaders said. "There will never be any life growing in your womb. You'll never experience the miracle of birth. You'll never hold your newborn in your arms. Nobody will ever call you Mommy. You're going to be in a lot of emotional pain as the reality sinks in."

That was supposed to help us? There was some truth to the statement—the fact was I hadn't had children, so I wouldn't experience the benefits of having children—but I couldn't see the point in lamenting a decision I wouldn't and couldn't change. Many women suffer depression during menopause—hormonal imbalances make it almost inevitable—mothers or no. I yearned for a more positive spin on the realities of menopause, a discussion that would focus on all I gain rather than what I lose. Looking around the room at the dozens of teary-eyed women, I felt determined to find the positive in menopause.

I finally found it in a wonderful seminar which treated menopause as a normal transition, a rite of passage to be celebrated, not mourned. The seminar leader was a yoga instructor; the participants were highly intelligent women who had devoted themselves to leading healthy lives, both mind and body. We shared incredibly personal stories and poems. We lit candles and incense, and chanted together, welcoming the wisdom that would come with this next phase of womanhood. I've never felt stronger.

Menopause did symbolize a change for me, but not the one my peers or society expected. Instead of questioning the choice I made a long time ago, I celebrated where I stood right there and then. Instead of fearing a past decision, I welcomed the wisdom of my own body and spirit. I reached for inner compassion and acceptance. I didn't cave in to conform to some impossible ideal of womanhood which didn't fit for me. Instead, I welcomed all that my choice had offered me, and appreciated all I had experienced. I checked in on my life to see if it was enjoyable as it existed. It didn't take long to see I loved my life. I loved teaching, coming home to Jim, preparing a fragrant stew on a cold night, baking apples with a hint of cinnamon, sharing holidays with my family and friends, playing with my dog, sleeping as late as I wanted on the weekends, planning vacations we could afford and not worrying about the important needs and wants of another human in our home.

My biological clock had, thankfully, stopped ticking.

9

Stepmother

I am a mother. It's not a pretty story, and it doesn't begin with the usual swollen belly, baby shower, friendly arguments over baby names and, finally, frantic urgings of "Push!" Rather, Jim presented me with two girls ages eight and twelve from his previous marriage. I now hold the legal title of stepmother.

When I learned that Jim had daughters, there was a brief moment in which I doubted my desire to marry him. I had made the choice not to have children; now, suddenly, at age fifty, I would have them. The prospect turned my world upside-down. Was I ready—and more importantly, was I willing—to change my mind about the most important decision I had ever made, a decision which had, for better or worse, altered the course of my life? I was aware of the awesome responsibility I would take on in terms of time, money, and energy. I considered the fact that children could place significant strain on a relationship, and wondered if Jim and I would be up to the challenge. I also considered what a wonderful experience stepmothering could be. I thought it might feel something like being an aunt. I enjoyed the time I spent with my niece and nephew and, at the end of the day, was happy to deliver them back into the loving care of their parents and return to the peace of my childfree home. I hoped it would be the same with Jim's daughters. I knew that, no matter for how long they visited with us, ultimately they would return to their mother's home where they lived. She was the custodial parent, and thank goodness for that. As open-minded as I was trying to be, the thought of a 24-hour-a-day child-centered home left me biting my fingernails to the quick.

Having never been a mother or stepmother before, I didn't know exactly what to expect, so I simply did what most women do: chose to believe that everything would work out for the best. Of course there would be challenges—that was part of the job description—but I felt I could overcome anything. I could do this! I would do this! After all, wasn't I a great teacher? Didn't my students value me? Why shouldn't my stepdaughters value me too?

I thought about the 1998 movie *Stepmom* with Julia Roberts and Susan Sarandon in which a blended family works through the various difficulties of adjusting to life together. Their success is largely due to perseverance, trial and error, and humor: lots of humor, side-splitting humor. We would also laugh together, I decided, and in this way, establish authentic, open lines of communication. I looked forward to the positive impact I could have on these girls' lives.

Armed with thoughts about my own stepfather and how much I treasured him, I continued to date Jim, excited about the relationship's possibilities. I didn't know what would happen, but decided that Jim was worth the risk.

For the first time, I felt at peace with a man. Jim knew how to listen. He treated me with the warmth, kindness, and respect that Jack and Warren had been incapable of giving me. We laughed a lot. We loved a lot. I began to fantasize about the life we would lead: me, Jim, and his daughters. I daydreamed about picnics in the park, elaborate family dinners, and loving kisses goodnight. I took a mental photo of the four of us standing close, arms around waists, wearing smiles that stretched from ear to ear. And simple as that, I was seduced by the myth of the perfect family.

Jim spoke with such love and joy about his two daughters. He warmed my heart with stories of caring for them as babies, encountering their first smiles, and watching them grow. Their antics were hilarious. Abbi loved to play dress-up, only she would dress up her father in women's clothing instead of herself! Carolyn had once snuck a tub of whipped cream from the refrigerator, and eaten it all in one sitting! They sounded like real characters. I was genuinely excited to meet them, and eager to get our happy family underway. Like anyone blinded by a fantasy, I dutifully ignored the potential for disappointment, and life's tendency to derail even the best laid plans.

When I first met eight-year-old Carolyn, I was struck by how cute she looked. She wore her blond hair in a high ponytail which accentuated her long face and doe-like eyes. She resembled her mother, with a small mouth and prominent nose. She had a dry sense of humor, like her father. Her voice wasn't loud, but deeper than one might expect of a young girl. But in other ways, she fit the profile. Give her candy—her favorite food group—and she bounced off the walls.

Abbigail looked like Jim. Her hair was dark, a warm brown with natural golden highlights; her skin olive. She wore a serious expression almost all of the time: her mouth turned downwards at the corners, her brow wrinkled. At twelve years old, she seemed to be developing permanent scowl lines between her eyes. I tried hard, but could never quite figure out what was going on behind that penetrating stare of hers.

In the beginning I didn't have much to do with the girls. Jim took full advantage of their visits to our home, spending quality time with them whenever he could. I would smile at the girls' squeals of laughter as they climbed onto their father's back, riding him like a pony. Over time, I became more involved with their visitations, and the problems began.

Abbi was angry at me from the outset. She took it upon herself to be as nasty as possible in my presence, making snide remarks and rejecting my efforts to connect. Carolyn, being younger and less independent, simply followed suit. Where was all of this anger coming from? I treated the girls well, opening my home to them and asking them questions in order to learn about their lives, so I knew it wasn't for lack of effort on my part. I assumed their anger was rooted in the shock of seeing their father with another woman, and hoped it would pass. I soon learned that that was not the case. Their mother, Marilyn, was working hard to turn her daughters against me. It worked. The girls saw me as the villain and their mother, the innocent victim of their father's selfish choices.

"Why did you date Marcia when you were still married to Mom?" the girls asked Jim regularly. (He and Marilyn had been separated at the time.) "Why doesn't Marcia have her own kids? It's because she hates them, isn't it?"

All Jim could do was answer with honesty, and hope that Marilyn would come to her senses and stop poisoning her children against their soon-to-be legal stepmother. Unfortunately, she never did.

All I could do was refute Marilyn's accusations through my actions, and hope that the girls would come to their own conclusions. In retrospect, I was doomed. How could I, a newcomer to the family, compete with the steady stream of lies being fed to them by their mother, whom they had loved and trusted for years? Still, I did what I could, convinced that I would teach my stepchildren to love me. Marilyn would see how much I gave to the girls, and I would win her over too. I pictured Marilyn and I bonded in our common goal of making Abbi and Carolyn happy. My bubble, for the time being, refused to burst.

I redoubled my efforts, struggling to find ways to keep the girls entertained. I would do anything to avoid hearing that dreaded statement: "I'm bored." The search for worthwhile amusements dominated mine and Jim's life. Where could we take them? What activities would they enjoy?

I tried to introduce them to things I had loved as a child, like classical music, to no avail.

"What is that shit?" Abbi said when I turned on the classical radio station in the car.

"Beautiful music," I answered, laughing nervously and wondering if I should comment on her foul language.

"Shut it off!" Abbi demanded. "Do you really think kids like that shit music?" At which point, she reached over and switched the station to some loud, non-melodic, dirge-like song with lyrics I couldn't distinguish (which was probably for the better since I'm sure I would have fainted).

She and her sister started singing loudly and rocking in their seats. I sat still and stewed, unsure if I should pull over and let Abbi know that this behavior was unacceptable, or let it go. I chose the latter, suffering in silence. The issue of discipline, I wasn't too clear on. Was I supposed to reprimand the girls, or should that be left to Jim? In the end, I took the easy way out, ignoring their bad behavior instead of taking the opportunity to teach them how to communicate wants and needs with respect. I wanted them to like me! I wanted them to tell their friends I was the best stepmom on the planet, not the dreaded stepmonster they couldn't stand. Of course, all the avoidance in the world wouldn't change how they viewed me.

In another desperate attempt to please, we took the girls to see the Nutcracker Ballet in New York City's Lincoln Center. They loved it, which was a relief, but I couldn't ignore the fact that those few hours of enjoyment had set us back hundreds of dollars. The tickets and food for four, not to mention gas and parking, had added up quickly. I saw the stark financial impact of that one excursion and wondered how parents could afford to treat their children to the new experiences they needed to flourish? After Jim lost his job and started his own business, we used my money to entertain, feed, and clothe the girls. I wanted to help, but sometimes resented the fact that my hard-earned money was going to my stepdaughters who didn't care for me at all.

My annoyance was mounting. No matter how hard I tried, Abbi and Carolyn simply refused to warm to me. Emotional outbursts in public had become routine. The girls would scream and cry, shout obscenities, and even throw food. I was reaching my limit. After a particularly messy food fight at a restaurant, I told Jim I wouldn't go out with the girls anymore. We had an argument, the first of many having to do with the girls' behavior. Caring for children had strained our relationship, just as I had feared.

Despite these challenges, Jim and I married on a rainy afternoon in November, standing in front of a roaring fire in a lovely restaurant, surrounded by our friends and family. His daughters were my bridesmaids. The officiate delivered a speech, honoring their role in our marriage. I continued to embrace the hope that time would heal all wounds, the myth that all families triumph in the end.

Being a stepmother wasn't all conflicts and heartbreak. There were amiable and fun times too. I enjoyed going to the girls' sporting events, woo-hooing from the bleachers alongside the other proud parents, sharing a thumbs-up when our kids did well. I had kids and now, after years of being different, I was accepted into the esteemed society of parents, and was no longer an "other." Some knew I was the girls' stepmother; others assumed I was their mom. It didn't matter. I was one of them.

However, that feeling was short-lived. The satisfaction of acceptance paled in comparison to the grief I dealt with daily. Stepparenting was everything I imagined parenting to be: an incredibly difficult job! Although the time off between visits helped, the deep hurt from the girls' bewildering reactions vibrated in my memory long after they had left our home.

Once, when Abbi delivered the "I'm bored" routine, I suggested we go to the library.

"Are you kidding me? Books?" she scoffed. "You don't have a clue about kids. Maybe it's because you have no kids. Actually, it's probably good. You'd be a really bad mother."

I looked at her and silently commiserated with animals who eat their young.

Was the fact that I didn't have children the reason I seemed to be failing as a stepmother? Maybe I would have known more if I had raised my own kids. Maybe I would have been better prepared. Maybe she was right!

I couldn't change the past, but I could influence the future. I set out to educate myself. I spoke with friends who had children and stepchildren. I read books on the subject. Jim and I talked endlessly. He assured me I was doing a great job. I didn't believe him. How could I when nothing I was doing was working? For me, being a stepmother meant working tirelessly to make everything right while everything got more and more wrong.

৩৩

As Abbi and Carolyn went on to high school then college, they withdrew from me and Jim even further, rather than getting closer as the myth promised.

"Give them space," all the professionals said. "When they leave their teens, they'll come to understand 'home.'"

The rift between us became a chasm despite our very best efforts. We never missed even one special event during their school years. We snapped photos at their graduations and displayed them on our mantle: there Jim was, there I was, beaming with pride. We were always invited to family parties, and we always attended. I credit Marilyn for that, although I wonder what was said after we left. We set up the girls' computers and helped clean their dorm rooms. Jim called them often, and visited with them when they came home for holidays and summer vacations. We took them with us on trips, and bought them gifts whenever we could. Still, they continued to pull away, Abbi especially.

Once both girls were successfully out of college, working steady jobs, and living on their own, I asked Jim if we might think about moving to Florida. During the long winter months on Long Island, I simply couldn't get warm! My hands and toes would turn red, threatening frostbite. I was often so cold, I felt dizzy. My mother, stepfather, sister and her family lived in Florida, and loved it. We visited often, dreaming of living there ourselves.

When I was offered a terrific retirement package, we knew the time had come. We made arrangements and told the girls. Carolyn congratulated us and said she looked forward to visiting. Abbi didn't take the news as well.

"How can you even think of leaving your own flesh and blood?" she asked testily. "Our family always stays together! What happens when I have kids? You won't be here to be their grandfather!" she wailed. I noticed I was absent from that statement; clearly, Abbi saw no place for me as her children's grandmother.

"We'll only be a plane ride away," Jim said. Then he assured her that we would remain active in her life and the lives of her children.

"Mom would never move away from us. Never!" she screamed. Clearly, her abandonment issues were coming up. Then she turned her anger toward me. "You're so selfish! You've always come before us! You're taking away my dad!"

And with that, she left. Jim and I never dreamed that that would be the last time we'd see her.

ᘯᘰ

Our beautiful new Florida home became a frequent destination for friends and family, Carolyn included. Sometimes she came with friends; oftentimes she came alone. Finally, I did what I should have done from day one: spent quality time alone with my gorgeous stepdaughter. She truly was a beauty. I have fond memories of picnicking on the beach, talking for hours with the warm sun beating on our bodies.

"This sandwich is the best I ever had!" she said. "Did you put cranberries in the turkey?" I loved her genuine reactions.

My connection with Carolyn continued. We both called and emailed regularly. I even helped her land a teaching job by training her in the art of the interview. She was grateful. It felt good. After all the years of heartache and disappointment, I finally felt successful and fulfilled as Carolyn's stepmother.

Unfortunately, I couldn't say the same for Abbi. She didn't visit, and she didn't call. She got engaged and didn't invite us to the wedding.

Yes, you read that right. We were not invited to our daughter's wedding.

Jim's fantasy of proudly walking his eldest daughter down the aisle came to an abrupt end. We tried to reconnect, sending Abbi and her fiancée plane tickets to Florida, along with a long letter expressing our heartfelt desire to be a part of their lives. We even offered to throw them an engagement party as a gesture of goodwill. They did call to thank us, but ultimately threw their plane tickets away.

Abbi's wedding day was one of the saddest in our lives. We remained in Florida, haunted by images of the celebration that was taking place without us. Jim agonized over who was walking his daughter down the aisle. How did she look? Was she happy? Did she miss him? Was she even thinking about him? Did she really hate him so much? Didn't she remember all those times he was there for her, all those times he had shown his love?

Abbi found a way to wound her father in the most vicious way. Carolyn eventually reverted to her old ways. At some point, she stopped responding to our communications. To this day, she refuses to speak to us. In the end, we were effectively severed from both Abbi's and Carolyn's lives. We'll never get used to this sad state of affairs. Our hearts ache because of it. Yet, there's a certain peace we now feel having given up the drama of parenthood. We've learned to think of Abbi and Carolyn with great love and compassion; we understand that any negative thoughts make us their victims. We wish them happiness, health, and full lives in the company of people who value them. I have mourned the loss of my stepdaughters. I've gone through the five stages of grief: denial, anger, bargaining, depression, and finally acceptance. I no longer suffer guilt, nor do I cling to the fantasy of being the consummate stepmother. I am at peace knowing I did the best I could do.

I learned a great deal from my experiences with Jim's daughters. Books didn't teach me. People didn't help me. Movies failed to show me the truth. I had to find out for myself that stepparenting, just like parenting, is steeped in myth. There is no such thing as a perfect family; we simply convince ourselves that there is by the stubborn refusal to acknowledge the reality of expectation and disappointment.

I signed on to stepparenting expecting an opportunity to bond with two children in a meaningful way. Jim's daughters meant the world to him. I wanted to be supportive of that sentiment by creating a loving, safe space in which Jim's daughters would grow. I looked forward to the rewards of stepparenting, the fulfillment of nurturing another human being's life. Those hopes, as it turned out, were based on unrealistic expectations. Those expectations were rooted in pronatalistic myths, myths which our society stubbornly perpetuates with no regard for the real-world consequences.

I paid a price for my foray into the world of parenting. I have experienced and continue to experience great pain over my stepdaughters' unwillingness to meet us halfway. Now that Abbi has sons—two boys ages five and eight, one of whom, we are told, looks just like Jim—Jim and I are grandparents, but we'll never get to fill those roles. Those boys don't even know we're alive.

Remember that hostile teacher I met thirty-six years ago at my first high school speaking engagement?

"It's all well and good now, not having kids," she had said. "How will you feel when you're old and alone with no one to take care of you? How will you feel without a grandchild to give you chocolate kisses?"

Well, I did have kids, and now I'm a grandmother. Having children promises a lifetime of love, right? If you do right by your children, they'll do right by you, isn't that true? Everything will work out for the best, won't it? I bought into it—me, the most unlikely of candidates—the myth was that strong.

So, now I ask you, where are my chocolate kisses?

10

No Regrets

I'm sitting in my screened-in enclosure at the back of our Florida home. The sun embraces me like a tender hug. I can hear my neighbor's wind chimes and smell the blooming jasmine in my garden. Two sandhill cranes glide toward the nearby nature preserve, emitting their characteristic trill. Their large, flapping wings move the still air. I always marvel at the abundance of life I encounter here. It's not uncommon to see bobcats, rabbits, raccoons, and armadillos. On summer nights, we're forced to close our bedroom's sliding door to shut out the cacophony of insects which makes sleep impossible.

I lay here with the hot summer sun on my body, drinking in the peace I relish. I'm practicing a visualization technique I read about somewhere, imagining the sunlight penetrating the surface of my skin to be absorbed by my aging bones. I imagine those bones getting stronger, armed with the vitamin D they need. I stubbornly refuse to be stooped over in my later years, bearing that telltale hump. I concentrate harder, sink deeper into my chaise lounge, and breathe a full sigh of sheer contentment.

Who am I kidding? Hump or no hump, sunlight or no sunlight, I *am* aging. Those brown spots on the tops of my wrinkled hands remind me, no matter how much vanishing cream I use or how many lotions and potions I slather all over my body, I'm not young anymore. I've noticed the start of ugly turkey waddle in my neck, and dimpled skin between my breasts. These unwelcome features seem to be worsening every day, or is it every hour ... or minute ... or second? Sometimes, I stand in front of the mirror and pull the skin of my face tight so I can't see the deep lines in my cheeks or the drooping eyelids. My hair has also thinned. I can't remember my natural color. Even my pubic hairs defy me: They're turning gray!

As I sit here, I think back on my 69 years on this planet. I made so many choices: pursuing the arts in my youth, becoming a teacher, marrying three men, and not having biological children. My love of piano got me into Manhattan's prestigious High School of Music and Art. Ballet gave me pleasure, sculpted calf muscles, and taught good posture. Although I can't say that all of my marriages were fulfilling, I learned important life lessons.

Was it the right choice for me not to procreate? Were all those finger-pointing tsk, tsk, tsking women and men right? Do I feel the way they warned me I would: sad, alone, worthless? Do I have regrets? I've been plagued by these questions for a long time. I wonder if parents have similar thoughts, fantasies about how their lives would be different had they chosen not to raise children.

I think about the teacher who attacked me in front of an auditorium full of impressionable teenagers, and many others who have echoed that ominous warning about ultimately regretting my choice. "Think of the chocolate kisses!" they urged. They meant well—most of them anyway. Their hearts and heads were overrun with fear, both of me (I was different) and for me (they thought I'd end up alone). Many were also jealous of my freedom.

"I'm tired of hearing your travel stories," one friend revealed. "And knowing you can sleep late every weekend, or afford a massage. Frankly, it's not fair!"

There are distinct advantages to not raising children. Still, most people genuinely believed I would miss the experience of motherhood. I wish I had been as upfront about my feelings as they were about their own, but I never had the courage to ask the uncomfortable question I was burning to ask: "What guarantees that your own kids will be there as you age?"

I remember visiting my aging aunt in an assisted living facility. The smell of urine, feces, and loneliness assailed my nostrils every time. I saw many people sitting alone and talking to themselves; slumped in a wheelchair, sedated to the point of near unconsciousness; or asleep in their beds, curled up tight as if willing themselves to disappear. I assumed many of them had children. So where were they? Some probably lived too far away. Some couldn't afford to travel, or were busy raising children of their own. Some had broken relationships with their now sick parents, eroded by time and a lack of willingness to change. Some of the elderly I encountered may have been guilty of abusing or abandoning their children, and were now suffering the consequences of poor parenting. Only now, after having spent the majority of their lives raising their children, the false hopes, myths, and disappointments associated with that career had come clear.

According to a recent article in AARP's magazine, "The Stranger in Your Family" by Meredith Maran, cases of parent-child estrangement are on the rise. The contributing factors are multiple and varied. The point is that the act of bearing a child does not ensure love and respect from that child as the pronatalistic myth would have us believe. Even the most caring parents can be disappointed by pronatalism's many broken promises.

While I relax in this backyard enclosure, I remember many times I momentarily regretted not having my own child to nurture, usually after a particularly lovely shared experience with another person's child: my niece's adorable ballet recital, my nephew's high school graduation, or the wedding of a close friend's son. Nobody considers the various challenges and frustrations when they are wistfully thinking about having a child, just like parents don't fantasize about a childfree lifestyle when their parental lives are going well. It's usually after an upsetting experience that, for both parents and non-parents, the grass seems greener on the other side.

I believe my child would have been loved, and taught to be a free spirit with a good sense of self-respect. I would have shared my own passions: education, reading, writing, and environmentalism. I would have taken him or her to concerts, theater, and ballets, and hope these cultural experiences were appreciated. Of course my child would have made a mark in his or her lifetime. Nobody says, "My child will be a drug addict," or "My child will drop out of school." Neither do I in my fantasies of the child I never conceived.

I've suffered guilt from a Jewish religion and culture which told me it was my duty to replenish the world after the unconscionable loss of human life in the Holocaust. Did I let my grandfather down by not naming children after his siblings who were brutally murdered?

If I had tried to conceive and discovered I couldn't, that at least would have been easier to explain. I doubt, however, that it would have excused me from the ever-present pressure to procreate. I imagine I would have been reminded, with a not-so-gentle nudge, of the options available to me: adoption, in vitro fertilization, or surrogacy birth. Pronatalism never stops.

Yet, when I attained the title of stepmother, I clearly saw how my own expectations and strong desire to be an effective stepparent to two beautiful young women were doomed by harsh reality. My daughters were far too angry and confused to let me in, and I was too hurt and let down to know what to do about it. It didn't matter how much I wanted to reach them. It was never going to happen, and it never did.

When it comes to parenting—and life in general—there are no guarantees. Every day parents are faced with realities that may not be consistent with societal promises. How many of my own friends and family faced problems with their own children? Many. How many of them have come to me in tears, sharing painful experiences of frustration, worry, or anger? Many. How many of them have been hurt, frightened, bewildered, overwhelmed, or terribly disappointed by the day-to-day realities of parenting? One friend thought she was funny when she said, "No kids? Are you kidding? What have you done for aggravation?"

Life is all about choices and consequences. Without a doubt, I've missed some wonderful moments as a result of my decision not to have children. However, haven't many parents missed myriad opportunities due to the lifestyle they chose? If I share the memories of my exhilarating seventeen-day East Kenya safari, trips to England, France, Spain, Italy, Greece, Ireland, Scotland, Switzerland, Chile, Argentina, Brazil and Hawaii, or the simple joys of sitting here in my own outdoor space enjoying the jasmine I planted, it would sound so trivial next to parents' memories. You can't equate growing a garden to raising a human. I wouldn't even dare.

Having a child is a lifetime commitment. I laugh when I hear people say, "I want to have kids when I'm younger. That way, when they leave the house at eighteen, I can have my life back."

In these days of economic challenges and over-indulged kids, your children may be staying home a lot longer; maybe forever! If they have children, those grandchildren will most likely play a part in your life. Not every grandchild gives chocolate kisses. Many can give enormous headaches, heartaches, and sadness. I've heard anguished grandparents tell of their grandchildren who steal, struggle with addictions, or never call. My own husband has two grandchildren he doesn't even know because of his defiant oldest daughter who believes she's getting back at us by keeping our grandchildren away.

For many, arriving at the decision not to have children is uncomplicated. They feel sure, they tell their friends and family, and that's that. It's not for them! Period. End of discussion. I envy those people. For me, it wasn't that easy.

In 1974, who had the courage to make that choice easily? The myth of mom and apple pie reigned supreme: the mother as angelic homemaker, the nuclear family as perfection. TV shows depicted having children as the consummate joy of a well-meaning, fulfilled life. All problems could and would be solved within a half-hour timeframe. In a paternalistic society that, for women, valued motherhood above all else, of course I would fear that I had made the wrong choice. If I had been wrong about playing the piano, so what? If teaching had been wrong for me, so what? If a marriage didn't work, so what? On to the next possibility! However, as the years came and went, the tick, tick, ticking of my biological clock seemed to intensify. My advancing age was a constant reminder that my eggs were dwindling; my body becoming increasingly unfit for childbirth and child-rearing. As the media exposed more and more stories about women happily conceiving in their 40s, 50s, and even 60s, I started re-questioning. Maybe it wasn't too late? Maybe I could now accept the career I had always resisted? It seemed as if the ticking of that clock would never end.

Surely, today's woman is different and society is different from how it was in 1974, but not as different as we'd like to believe. The same expectations and pressures exist—find a man, get married, have children—only now we pretend that they don't.

I recently responded to a woman who posted a favorable response on my blog. "I'm honored to hear from a pioneer of childfreedom," she wrote back. "Thanks for all you've done."

Her comment startled me. I've been called many things in the last seventy years—friendly, compassionate, driven, goofy, brazen, argumentative, and sometimes courageous—but I've never heard "pioneer." Me, a pioneer? My mom certainly was as a business owner in the '50s. She was an enigma, pushing against the ideals of the time. But me, a pioneer because I've advocated for those who don't want to raise children?

I wondered if more people would feel the way this woman does. Would my life's story be of interest? I'm not a movie star. I have no claim to fame other than my fifteen minutes on *60 Minutes*. Do people now look at this topic and think, "Shit! Glad I wasn't living during her repressive time. I don't need to read this memoir. I'm fine with not having kids. I feel no pressure"? Maybe the question is not whether I'm a pioneer but rather whether we need a pioneer at all.

The answer is yes. Increased acceptance of the choice not to have kids is not full acceptance. It doesn't mean that childfree women are no longer considered selfish monsters, just that less people consider them so. The sad truth is that we have yet to break free from the bonds of societal expectation. We've come a long way towards eradicating pronatalism and we've still got a long way to go.

We are taught that the desire to parent is instinctive. For those of us who don't feel the pull towards having children, we wonder if there's something wrong with us biologically, mentally, or emotionally. We must disappoint our own parents who wish for nothing more than to know the feeling of holding their grandchild. After all the years and hard work of raising us, they feel they have the right to claim the title of Grandma or Grandpa.

"Grandchildren are the rewards of parenting," I've often heard, or "Wait! Just wait till you have kids of your own! Then you'll know what we faced."

And why wouldn't they feel this way? They are inundated with advertising which features adorable children even when the product being sold has nothing to do with kids. Movie stars are depicted on the covers of countless magazines holding their precious, beautifully clothed children. Songs preach the joys of parenthood, butterfly kisses and quality time, and how having a baby is a wonderful way to express love. Bridal showers are replete with baby gifts, failing to acknowledge the fact that the bride may not want or be able to have children. Soap operas tout pregnancy as the definitive way to heal all marital problems. An only child will ask his parents for siblings because he's the only one in his class who doesn't have them. Friends ask friends when the next child is planned. If the friend has daughters, won't she try for a boy? If she has only one child, doesn't she want another?

Frankly, self-doubt has reared its ugly head many times over the years. Yet, I would rather have spent this time questioning my choice than have had children knowing it was wrong. I simply did not want the responsibility; that felt right for me. When I feel the need to be with children, I can embrace my niece and nephew, or welcome the students I've taught to whom I remain connected. I can volunteer to be a foster grandmother, or mentor a needy child. I can be a Girl Scout leader, or get involved with another worthy organization like The Humanists of the Treasure Coast, which grows community gardens to help feed hungry children.

The decision not to have children gave me what I needed for 69 years, and I have no doubt that that fulfillment will continue into my 70s and 80s. In my opinion, that choice is not fairly taught. Have you ever heard about the advantages of a child-free lifestyle? When I tried to share that perspective with a high school class, I faced the wrath of picketing parents. I doubt that my reception would be much warmer today. There are no courses challenging us to ask if we are really parent material. There are no tests posing questions about knowledge of parenting. There are no support systems for those who honestly say, "No, I don't want children." Instead, we are labeled as hedonistic, unloving, and selfish. It doesn't matter how aggressively we devote ourselves to our jobs, causes, or communities. It doesn't matter how many lives we touch in other meaningful ways. In the eyes of society, we are different, and therefore threatening. I ask you this: As long as people live meaningful and personally fulfilled lives, is not having a child really so awful?

Yesterday, one of my forever students came to visit. Her sweet little girl ran into my arms with the exuberance and delicious charm of her short four years on this planet. (She knows I delight in her company. We've spent hours together watching cartoons and eating ice cream while I baby-sat.) Her warm little arms encircled my back as I scooped her up. Although my back hurt, I didn't let her down. She nuzzled her face into my neck, and I smelled a mixture of Play-Doh and baby powder. She gave me a big kiss. I felt something wet and sticky on my cheek.

"Hanna, why do I feel something sticky?" I laughed.

"I just ate a chocolate bar!" she squealed.

Did that chocolate kiss feel less than it would have if she were a blood child or grandchild?

As I sit on my chaise lounge watching a butterfly try to find the perfect flower, hearing my husband Jim speaking on the phone, warmed by the sun, touched by my memories, I'm looking forward to whatever life brings next. I want to take Salsa lessons, learn how to swim, and play golf. (How have I lived in Florida for ten years without knowing how to swim or play golf?) I'm gathering information for our next trip. It may be a cruise down the Amalfi Coast of Italy in a romantic sailing ship, or a tour of our Northwest national parks. I need to plant some more tomato plants, having lost my summer crop to the ravages of the hot Florida summer sun. Jim and I are going to a jazz concert this weekend. My sister and I have purchased season tickets to the Kravis Center for the Performing Arts in West Palm Beach. On those days, we look forward to eating homemade scones with clotted cream in a nearby teahouse after the performance. I want our gardeners to transplant a beautiful hibiscus plant from the back to the front of our home. I'm planning to teach our gardeners' wives how to speak English. We can afford a housekeeper, so I never have to wash another toilet or mop the kitchen floor. Instead, I'm free to relax in my hot tub or read a book. I'm searching for plane tickets to attend the wedding of one of my forever students this May. I'm looking forward to learning what career my nephew chooses, and if my niece feels content in hers. I'm considering a new color for our master bathroom walls—something bright and sunny—and interviewing contractors to remodel our kitchen. I just finished my first knitted sweater. Now, I'll look for a music school where I can learn to play jazz.

My life is full, rich, and rewarding. We aren't wealthy but live a comfortable lifestyle. Without children to support, we've managed to save some money that should last and allow us to sustain the lifestyle to which we've become accustomed. Our Florida home, situated in a full-service gated community, has four bedrooms which afford us more than enough space. There's our bedroom, a room devoted to Jim's passion for model trains, an office for me, and a guestroom reserved for family and friends who visit during those long, cold winter months in New York.

As a retired English teacher, words fascinate me. Where do they come from? What do they mean? How are they used? Recently, I researched the word "birth." I discovered that it finds its origins in the Old Norse word "byrth," which means "to bear." I also found these synonyms: commencement, source, delivery, beginning, any coming into existence; as expected, the word is commonly associated with babies and the miracle of life. I've never given birth to a child, but I have birthed many things which have made my life deliciously sweet:

Love, to my many wonderful students. Support, to these students and their parents in times of need. Education, through my teaching, of course, but also through unique initiatives like "We Care," an outreach program I developed for my school encouraging American families to embrace international families. I'm proud to report that that program evolved into a yearly event, "International Night," during which international children and parents share art, song, and dance from their respective cultures. Mr. Khan, the father of one of my ESL students, lovingly shared a Persian rug his mother had given him before he left Pakistan.

"This is the last thing I have from my mama," he said in halted English, tearing up at the memory of leaving his beloved mother behind.

I created "Speeches from the Heart," an opportunity for my students to share with their peers what they endured leaving their native countries for ours. I'll never forget the tears streaming down the faces of 200 middle school children and their teachers when Evelina, a shy Polish girl, announced, "Don't tell me you're my friend because you wave at me in the hall. Prove it! Call me, or invite me to your home on the weekend. Help me with my homework. Sit next to me in the lunchroom. Stop making fun of my accent." By the time she finished speaking, she was weeping. None of the students laughed. Many became real friends to Evelina.

I'm on the board of The Humanists of the Treasure Coast, an organization of people who are ethical in their beliefs but not traditionally religious. We offer support to parents who seek to raise their children as ethical humanists. In this way, I'm helping to erase the stereotype that non-religious people are worthless— one which strikes close to home.

Finally, I've given birth to a book. It's taken a lifetime to make the confessions that appear in these pages. Even now, I fear those readers who may harbor resentment, or try to punish me for my personal choice. Let me be clear: My goal is not to aggravate, but rather to educate and inspire, and in so doing, erase the dangerous influence of pronatalism from our society. I can only hope that in these first two aims, I've succeeded. As for the last, we'll have to wait and see. And as for me, I can enjoy my life to the fullest knowing, once and for all, that I made the right choice. I am a childless—no, childfree—woman. I have no regrets.

Appendix A:
Volunteer and Donation
Opportunities with Youth
Organizations

ArtBridge Houston (www.artbridgehouston.org): A unique Texas organization helping homeless and "at risk" children through the joy of art. ArtBridge encourages self-expression and nurtures imagination.

Asante Africa Foundation (www.asanteafrica.org): Builds and secures physical infrastructures for all children attending school in Tanzania and Kenya. Provides teaching resources and educational materials, and offers scholarships and sponsorships for highly motivated and academically gifted children.

Big Brothers Big Sisters (www.bbbs.org): The nation's largest donor-supported mentoring network, matching children in need (ages 6-18) with volunteer mentors.

Boy Scouts of America (www.scouting.org): Providing direction to boys in a carefully orchestrated character-building program which prepares them for the responsibilities of adulthood. (Note: If your personal religious preferences are agnostic, atheist, or humanist, you may not feel at home here. The Boy Scouts of America insists that their boys and leaders acknowledge a God)

Boys & Girls Clubs of America (www.bgca.org): Provides a loving, safe environment for children lacking in adult care and supervision. Takes volunteers of all ages.

CASA for Children (www.casaforchildren.org): A Court Appointed Special Advocate (CASA) is a volunteer chosen by a judge to watch over and advocate for children removed from their homes due to parental abuse and neglect.

Children's Grief Center (www.childrensgrief.org): A non-profit organization offering grief counseling to children in New Mexico.

Children's Path (www.childrenspath.com): Supports the social, emotional and intellectual development of underserved children and youth in California schools and agencies.

Child's Play (www.childsplaycharity.org): Dedicated to improving the lives of children through toys and games.

Dance Chance (www.springfieldballet.org/outreach.aspx): Funded by a grant through the Community Foundation of the Ozarks, Dance Chance allows schools to provide students with free lessons, dance wear, ballet shoes and tickets to ballet performances.

Florida Guardian ad Litem Program (www.guardianadlitem. org): A Guardian ad Litem advocates for a child in legal proceedings. Use this website to volunteer your time to help represent a voiceless child.

Girl Scouts of America (www.girlscouts.org): Helping girls discover the fun, friendship and power of girls united. (Note: The Girl Scouts are less strict than the Boy Scouts about the acknowledgement of a God)

Hugs and Hope (www.hugsandhope.org): Sending "Happy Mail" to sick children to provide them a few more smiles, a little more hope, and a reason to get out of bed each day.

Junior Achievement (www.ja.org): Volunteers share their experiences to inspire, prepare and empower children by teaching them the importance of goals, entrepreneurship, and financial literacy and responsibility.

KaBOOM! (www.kaboom.org): Builds safe playgrounds in areas lacking the funds to do so. Since its inception in 1995, KaBOOM! has led over 1,500 playground construction projects that pair community leaders with funding partners who support their mission.

Kids Against Hunger (www.kidsagainsthunger.org): A humanitarian food organization dedicated to eradicating world hunger through feeding hungry children in the USA and beyond.

Legitimate Charities (www.legitimatecharities.com): Provides information on which charities will put your donations to good use, and tips on how to avoid scams.

Little League Online (www.littleleague.org): Provides information on how to volunteer to be a Little League coach or manager.

Locks of Love (www.locksoflove.org): A public non-profit organization that provides hairpieces to financially disadvantaged children in the United States and Canada under age 21 suffering from long-term medical hair loss from any diagnosis.

Make-a-Wish Foundation (www.wish.org): Enriching the lives of children with life-threatening medical conditions through its wish-granting work. Volunteers serve as wish granters, fundraisers, special events assistants and in numerous other capacities.

Mr. Holland's Opus Foundation (www.mhopus.org): Inspired by the film of the same name, the Mr. Holland's Opus Foundation donates new and used instruments to schools and music programs that lack adequate financial resources. (Note: This organization is near and dear to my heart. One of my own mentors, Gabriel Kosakoff, reached out to help me in high school during a vulnerable time. We're still united in friendship. He was my beloved teacher at The High School of Music & Art, now known as the Fiorello H. LaGuardia High School of Music & Art and Performing Arts, located in Lincoln Center, NY. Although retired, he spends enormous energy with this foundation to promote the joy of music in areas sorely in need of musical instruments. As my father used to say, "Music vibrates in your soul long after the last note is heard.")

National Mentoring Partnership (www.mentoring.org): Matches mentors with children ages 6-18 who lack meaningful relationships with adults.

Pajama Program (www.pajamaprogram.org): Providing new pajamas and books to children in need around the world, many of whom are awaiting adoption.

Peace Links (www.peace-links.org): Volunteers work with children and young adults to develop conflict resolution skills, share creative arts, or pursue research projects in Sierra Leone, Africa.

Rainbows (www.rainbows.org): An international charity dedicated to helping youth navigate the grief process, including the death of a parent or loved one, divorce, and the deployment or incarceration of a family member.

Reading is Fundamental (www.rif.org): Reaching underserved children from birth to age 8, RIF gives away nearly 15 million books each year, operating out of nearly 17,000 locations across the country.

Ronald McDonald House Charities (www.rmhc.org): Provides a home away from home for families who can't afford to pay for lodging near a hospitalized child.

Save the Children (www.savethechildren.org): A worldwide organization dedicated to helping impoverished children throughout the world. Through financial sponsorship, caring individuals are matched with children in need to fund projects that make a real and sustainable difference.

Sema Project (http://semaacademy.wordpress.com/): Donates money and supplies to the Sema Academy, a school of 300 students in southwestern Kenya.

Senior Corps, Foster Grandparent Program (www.seniorcorps.gov/): If you're 55 or older and want to serve as a foster grandparent, this organization will place you where you're most needed in your community.

Smile Train (www.smiletrain.org): Providing surgery for children around the world suffering from cleft palates. Surgeries costs as little as $250.

Special Olympics (www.specialolympics.com): An international organization and competition held every two years (alternating between Winter and Summer Games) for children and young adults with intellectual challenges.

St. Jude (www.stjude.org): A widely-respected research hospital for pediatric treatment of cancer and other catastrophic illnesses. They never turn any child away.

UNICEF (www.unicefusa.org): A well-respected international organization providing children with health care, clean water, nutrition, education, protection, emergency relief, and more. The U.S. Fund for UNICEF supports UNICEF's work through fundraising, advocacy and education in the United States.

Vitamin Angels (www.vitaminangels.org): Provides essential nutrients, especially vitamin A, to infants and children under 5 years of age.

Voices for America's Children (www.voices.org): The nation's largest network of multi-issue child advocacy organizations, they lead advocacy efforts at the community, state and federal levels to improve the lives of all children, especially those most vulnerable, and their families.

We're Talking (www.pamf.org/teen/about): A crisis intervention program comprised of physicians, social workers, educators and researchers concerned with addressing the health care needs of adolescents.

Appendix B
Support Organizations and
Resources for Childfree People

Childfree Reflections (www.childfreereflections.blogspot.com): My own blog.

Babes Without Babes (www.babeswithoutbabes.com): A group of women 35 and older who do not have children and want to connect with others living the same lifestyle.

ChildFree.net (www.childfree.net): A group of adults who share at least one common desire: they do not wish to have children of their own. Members are teachers, doctors, business owners, authors, computer experts—you name it.

ChildFree By Choice (www.facebook.com/home.php#!/group.php?gid=2227994458): A Facebook group for the childfree.

Child Free Zone (www.child-free-zone.blogspot.com): A Phoenix, AZ-based childfree group providing articles and information.

Childless By Choice (www.northvalley.net/cbc): This national organization educates and advocates for the positive aspects of remaining childfree, and provides support to those who are unable to have children of their own.

Childless By Choice Project (www.childlessbychoiceproject. com): Laura Scott, author of *Two is Enough*, heads this research project and documentary exploring the motives and decision-making process behind the choice to remain childfree.

Happily Childfree (www.happilychildfree.com): Contains frequently asked questions, reading lists and references for those searching for more information on "childfreedom."

Kidding Aside (www.kiddingaside.net): The world's first childfree organization actively campaigning for equal rights for the childfree.

Laura Carroll, author of *The Baby Matrix: Why Freeing Our Minds From Outmoded Thinking About Parenthood & Reproduction Will Create a Better World* and *Families of Two: Interviews with Happily Married Couples Without Children by Choice*. Author site (www.lauracarroll.com).

No Kidding (www.nokidding.net): An international social club for adult couples and singles who have never had children. No Kidding is non-political and non-religious.

No Kids Passion (www.nokidspassions.com): A free online dating and social networking site for singles who have no interest in having children.

Positively Childfree (www.positivelychildfree.com): A discussion board and forum for people who have chosen the childfree lifestyle.

World Childfree Association (www.worldchildfree.org): A nonprofit and volunteer organization supporting the childfree choice. Information on membership, news, activities and project updates are provided.

Acknowledgments

As a reader, I've always wondered why anyone would include this page. As a writer, I get it.

Having finished this memoir, I'm aware of the tremendous effort it took to get it into your hands. So reader, I hope you read this page.

First, there's my editor Justine Tal Goldberg, owner of WriteByNight. She convinced me to take a writing course she gave with her partner David Duhr. After reading a small piece about my choice not to have children, they cheered me on to write this book. Justine's sage advice, teaching and brutal honesty kept me going through many bouts of writer's block. She taught me that "revision" is not a dirty word.

To Daniel Kalder who helped with my book proposal and marketing plan, my heartfelt thanks and appreciation.

To Phyllis Bittel, your awesome massage therapy helped me through many months of rejection after rejection. Your hands and heart are special to me.

Next, there are all my friends and family members who took the time to read and share heartfelt reactions: Irene Reichert, Linda Ushkowitz, Marcia Reass, Gabe Kosakoff, Gail Less, Linda Gammin, Maida Feingold, Anu Delcourt, Rose Price, Vena Brown, Gloria Jacobovitch. My cyber-space buddies Elaine Nadalin and DeAnna D'Amelio, hearing you call me a "pioneer" in the childfree movement touched my spirit. To Jane

Evers, when you said, "You know what? This is a good book!" I felt there was hope. You never say what you don't feel. I'm blessed to say that there are too many people to list in full. You know who you are and why I love and treasure you in my life. To the late Ellen Peck, author of *The Baby Trap*, you were the first person who made me realize that parenting is a choice, not a destiny. Long after we're both gone, I hope others continue on the path we took to educate and inspire.

To my sister Robin Neandross, I want to say how much I love you. People are always saying, "Oh, it was your younger sister who stopped you from wanting kids." Never! Your presence in my life is one of the sweetest gifts I received from our mother and my beloved stepfather.

To Laura Carroll, author of *The Baby Matrix* and *Families of Two*, your encouragement and suggestions to use Lisa DeSpain for my formatting and Derek Murphy for my cover was a blessing.

Finally, to my husband Jim, I can't find the words to thank you. You're always here to help and love me. Your expertise in computers saved me from many crises of saving documents in "creative" ways so that I could never find them again! Your children were welcome additions to my life who taught me how rewarding and difficult stepparenting can be.

To those skeptics who were so concerned I had made the wrong choice, I'm glad you're reading this.

About the Author

Marcia Drut-Davis, B.S., M.S. in TESOL, is an outspoken advocate for parenting choices and past chapter president of the National Organization for Non-Parents. Prior to getting her master's degree at the age of 50 in TESOL, she taught common branch subjects in New York, California and Michigan. Her peers recognized her abilities, nominating her for the Walt Disney Company's American Teacher Awards in 1998. In 2000, she retired to Florida where she taught future teachers in the College of Education at Florida Atlantic University. Presently, she volunteers teaching English and literacy in a local library and is a bimonthly writer for the *Pineapple Post* in Jensen Beach. She lives with her husband Jim and a rescued 5-pound Chihuahua.

Made in the USA
San Bernardino, CA
23 December 2017